WORLD CUP NUGGETS

Published by Ockley Books Limited, Huddersfield, England

First published June 2018

This book is 100% unofficial, all figures
are taken from FIFA.com

ISBN - 978-1-910906-149

Layout & design by Michael Kinlan,
edited by David Hartrick

Printed & bound by:
Biddles Printing, King's Lynn

WORLD CUP NUGGETS

RICHARD FOSTER

OCKLEY BOOKS
.com

WORLD CUP NUGGETS

INTRODUCTION

As memorable birthdays go my tenth has always been hard to beat and remains firmly implanted in my psyche. Not that it is a memory of which I care to be reminded. On June 14 1970 in the shimmering heat of León, England were facing West Germany in the World Cup quarter final, a repeat of the Final four years earlier. Just like millions of English football fans I tuned in to watch our World Champions continue their dominance of international football.

It all felt so thrilling, so exotic to be watching a match live that was taking place over 5,500 miles away. A feeling that was reinforced by the unusual sight of black nets, to which I immediately took a fancy—a distinctive element of the overall aesthetic that was Mexico 1970. With the core of the 1966 side still very much part of the squad, England travelled with a justified sense of superiority. Gordon Banks, Bobby Moore, Alan Ball, Bobby Charlton, Geoff Hurst and Martin Peters were all there under the guidance of the wily, practical and successful Alf Ramsey.

A nation was fully expecting the team to overcome the Germans and a sneaking sense of invincibility was beginning to build, although it had been somewhat shaken by a narrow 1-0 loss in a group game to the exceptional Brazilian side. But this was now crunch time and having proved our strength in the previous tournament, progress was anticipated, nay assumed.

Such confidence was somehow emboldened with the team wearing the red shirts of 1966 as the Germans again wore white and even the ball was of a reassuringly orange hue. A repeat of that victory at Wembley was on the cards as fate had clearly decided this was going to be England's day. Despite the late withdrawal of Gordon Banks before the match with a stomach complaint, his deputy Peter Bonetti had made six international appearances previously and only conceded one goal so we were in safe hands. Furthermore this squad had shown how to recover from adversity as had been proven by Moore, the captain, who was at his imperious best in the group games despite the worrying distraction of having been arrested in Colombia prior to the tournament for allegedly stealing some jewellery. The belief was that nothing could knock this team out of its stride.

When Alan Mullery's first and only goal for the national team put England in front with a neat finish at the near post after a searching cross from Keith Newton the natural order was in place. Just after half-time Martin Peters did what he was famous for as he ghosted in beyond the far post to double the lead. 2-0 up and England coasting into the semi-finals felt pretty good and would be the perfect way for me to celebrate reaching double figures.

Both goals could have been saved if German keeper Sepp Maier had been a bit stronger but we cared not a jot. However, goalkeeping fallibility was soon to rear its ugly head as Bonetti then came under scrutiny and failed the examination. In the 69th minute Franz Beckenbaeur's long-range shot lacked venom but slithered under Bonetti's dive. Ramsey's response was to use the newly introduced substitution system to take off Bobby Charlton immediately after the first German goal, apparently to save his legs for the semi-final.

But when Use Seeler's ridiculous back header looped agonisingly over Bonetti into the far corner, the forlorn keeper's reaction was one of disbelief as he just looked at the diminutive Seeler. That disbelief was shared by his defenders and all of us at home as the Chelsea keeper's vulnerability was cruelly exposed, the fact that he was not wearing gloves made him look all the more hapless and weak. Bonetti did not get a chance to redeem himself as this was his last appearance in an England shirt.

Seeler's equaliser to make it 2-2 ensured the game went to extra time in the searing Mexican heat. Still we had been here before as Kenneth Wolstenholme reminded us in the commentary "as they were in the World Cup Final of 1966, and if history is to repeat itself then England will score two goals." If only. Of course Gerd Müller put the final nail in the coffin when he hooked the ball past Bonetti from close range for the Germans' third, decisive goal. Once the true awfulness of what had happened sank in I cried, quite a lot, and the birthday cake my mother had prepared tasted of bitter disappointment.

Although I did not know this at the time while wallowing in my personal hell, this was preparation for the misery that would ensue over the next four decades of failure and decline. Little did I know that this would be the start of a run that would see the Germans finish ahead of England for eleven successive World Cups and counting. As a counter balance I wish I could dredge up some memory of the previous tournament but I was just too young to do so.

Although I was six when England won the World Cup I cannot remember any details about the tournament or even the final itself, which I watched with my elder brother on our black-and-white television. What did make a much more lasting impression was going to the cinema to watch *Goal! The World Cup,* the official film that documented the events of 1966. As the posters screamed with customary hyperbole 'See it on the Big Colour Screen!' and it was that splash of colour that captured the imagination. The red of England's shirts in the Final, the orangeness of the ball plus the mixture of red, white and blue provided by the thousands of Union Jacks in the crowd. This was a sensory overload and quite intoxicating for a child who was used to monochrome.

What I did not realise at the time was the excellent commentary that accompanied the film was by none other than Brian Glanville, a man who I came to respect as one of the greatest football writers of modern times. He is also responsible for writing *The Story of the World Cup*, the definitive history of the tournament and his updated editions are the first port of call when researching any book and this one in particular. There is no point in attempting to emulate Glanville's masterpiece and this book is certainly not intended to do that.

What this book aims to do is to bring to light some of the oddities, idiosyncrasies and quirks of the World Cup, of which there have been plenty in the 20 tournaments held since 1930. I have used a variety of sources including Glanville's comprehensive tome and excellent reference books such as Nick Holt's *Mammoth Book of the World Cup* and a special mention to Simon Gleave, Head of Analysis, Gracenote Sports for his invaluable contribution. Many thanks to all those who helped me discover the following nuggets.

1930

HOST
Uruguay

CITIES
Montevideo (Three Stadia)

DEBUTANTS
Argentina, Belgium, Bolivia,
Brazil, Chile, France, Mexico,
Paraguay, Peru, Romania,
Uruguay, USA, Yugoslavia

FINAL
Wednesday 30 July, Estadio Centenario (80,000)

URUGUAY (1) 4
Dorado, Cea, Iriarte, Castro

V

ARGENTINA (2) 2
Peucelle, Stábile
(Half-time score in brackets)

TOTAL ATTENDANCE
590,544 over 18 matches (Average 32,808)

TOP GOALSCORER (8)
Guillermo Stábile, Argentina

"I LIKED THE FINAL GAME BECAUSE IT WAS A TOUGH ONE, AS I BELIEVE FOOTBALL SHOULD BE - A GAME FOR STRONG AND HEALTHY MEN."

Jules Rimet

INTRODUCTION

When Jules Rimet first conceived of the idea for a World Cup it is highly unlikely that he would have envisaged quite how it popular it would become in 2018 or that he would end up travelling on the SS Conte Verde to Uruguay in 1930, the same ship that carried the Belgian, Romanian and French teams and also picked up the Brazilians en route to Montevideo. The Yugoslavs, the fourth European team to take part, literally missed the boat as it was fully booked by the time they agreed to enter and so they had to undertake a separate voyage.

Rimet was originally inspired to establish the tournament to complement the Olympic football tournament, which was the premier international football competition at the time, but which was only open to amateurs. With the 1932 Olympic Games set for Los Angeles the organising committee took the decision to drop football as the Americans could not get their head around a sport that had not taken off in their country as it had in the rest of the world, thus creating the opportunity for the World Cup to fill the gap.

Almost 90 years later there is no doubting that the football World Cup is the biggest sporting occasion on the globe. The overall television audience for the 2014 Finals was a staggering 3.2 billion, which equates to ¾ of the world's total population. One billion people watched the final in the Maracanã. In contrast the Super Bowl, which is often touted as one of the challengers to the World Cup final as a mass spectacle, attracts just over 10% of the audience with 110 million viewers watching the 2018 contest between the Philadelphia Eagles and the New England Patriots. This is mere bagatelle in comparison.

HOSTS

Uruguay were chosen as hosts for the inaugural tournament for a variety of reasons including the fact that they were unofficial world champions, having won the previous two Olympic tournaments in 1924 in Paris and 1928 in Amsterdam. It was an impressive achievement considering 1924 was the first time they entered the Olympics. Furthermore those two gold medals are the only ones Uruguay have ever won, ensuring that the players are considered sporting heroes to this day. They were clearly in pole position to make home advantage count when the World Cup was held in Montevideo. Coincidentally the 1930 World Cup final between Uruguay and Argentina was a repeat of the 1928 Olympic final.

The decision was also ameliorated by the fact that the Uruguayan FA were so keen to attract the very best European countries they were willing to pay for the travel and hotel expenses of those invited. This magnanimous gesture did not prove that popular with European giants such as Austria, Hungary, Germany or Italy gave the cold shoulder to the overtures of the Uruguayans and FIFA by staying at home. England were not even on the invitee list as they and the other home nations were in the middle of one of several stand-offs with FIFA and were left in cold isolation. A late, desperate invitation was shunned.

To celebrate being the host of the inaugural tournament the Uruguayans were determined to make the most of being centre stage and commissioned a new stadium to be built in Montevideo. The Estadio Centenario, so called because it was celebrating 100 years of Uruguay's independence from Brazil, boasted an impressive capacity of 90,000 that dwarfed the other two stadia being used for the World Cup, which were more modest club grounds. Although building the Centenario was a bold statement of intent there were a series of teething problems that would set an unwanted precedent for future World Cups when the thorny issue of missed construction deadlines would raise its head on a depressingly frequent basis.

After heavy rain delayed the unveiling of the stadium and with the race against time lost, the consequence was that the first ever game played in World Cup history was a rather low key affair as the host nation were not involved. Uruguay were still waiting for their showpiece stadium to be finished so the honour of christening the World Cup fell to France and Mexico who played at the much more humble Estadio Pocitos, home to Peñarol. This was a stadium and a match that did not capture the imagination of the locals and the smaller capacity was not tested.

The attendance was more a mathematically pleasing figure than a sign of any great popularity, as 4,444 witnessed the arrival of the World Cup on 13th July. That figure remains among the lowest crowds in World Cup finals history but it was by no means the smallest. That feat was achieved just two days later when only 300 hardy souls dribbled into the same stadium for Peru's game against Romania, a miserable total that would be a disappointment for a team in the ninth tier of English football let alone the leading international tournament. Not only is it the lowest recorded attendance at a World Cup finals but it is also the only occasion that a crowd of fewer than a thousand people have attended a World Cup finals match.

Despite the indifference of the citizens of Montevideo it was entirely appropriate that France should be one of the combatants in the opening match as the idea of the World Cup was the brainchild of two Frenchmen, not only the celebrated Jules Rimet but also fellow FIFA official Henri Delaunay. Rimet and Delaunay must have been immensely proud that the first player to score a goal in the World Cup Finals was fellow countryman Lucien Laurent in the 19th minute of that very first game. Laurent's tournament was cut short in their second group match when he suffered a serious ankle injury after a rough challenge from Argentinian Luis Monti, of whom more later. Considering Laurent only made ten appearances for France in his whole career and scored one other goal for the national team, he was clearly the right man in the right place.

Rimet and Delaunay would undoubtedly have afforded themselves a smile of satisfaction that as well as the first World Cup goal the last one scored in the 20th century was also by a Frenchman. Emmanuel Petit's late strike in the 1998 Final in Paris put the gloss on the French team's emphatic victory over Brazil as Zinedine Zidane lifted the trophy for the only time in the country's history. A fitting tribute to the two pioneers of the World Cup and it was also appropriate that Laurent was there to savour France's triumph, the only surviving member of the 1930 squad.

PLAYERS - BROTHERS IN ARMS

Laurent's elder brother, Jean also travelled with the French squad but did not get any minutes on the pitch. They were just one of four pairs of siblings on show in the 1930 Finals, with two sets playing for Mexico. Manuel and Felipe Rosas just pipped their countrymen Rafael and Francisco Garza Gutiérrez to the accolade of being the first brothers to appear together in a World Cup but all four played in their group match against Argentina, a feat that has not been emulated since. In the final the Argentinians also fielded a pair of brothers, Juan and Mario Evaristo. The Evaristos set the precedent for a surprisingly high number of siblings who would play together in the World Cup Final.

It was not until 1954 that another pair of brothers played in a World Cup final – Ottmar and Fritz Walter were in the victorious West German side and thus became the first brothers to win the trophy. Twelve years later Bobby and Jack Charlton repeated the trick when England beat West Germany at Wembley. The Dutch pair of René and Willy Van de Kerkhof hold the unique record of being selected for two consecutive World Cup final squads, although both ended in defeat in the final. Furthermore, having scored during the second round of games in 1978—Willy in the 5-1 victory over Austria and Rene four days later in a 2-2 draw with West Germany—they are the only twins to have scored at the same tournament.

The Italian Sala brothers, Patrizio and Claudio also featured at the 1978 tournament but they were not quite as prominent as the Van de Kerkhofs as they only played in the third placed play-off match.

If the Sala brothers were mainly bit part players, Vyacheslav and Viktor Chanovs were the definition of being on the sidelines. Both were goalkeepers in the Russian squad in 1982 but neither of them saw a minute's action, as they were back-up to the redoubtable Rinat Dasayev who was an ever-present in Spain. The tournament featured the last set of brothers to make the World Cup final a family affair; Bernd and Karlheinz Förster the German pair who played in the 1982 loss to Italy. Karl-Heinz then also played in the next final when Germany again lost, to Argentina. There was a third pair of brothers at the 1982 tournament. The Yugoslavs, Zlatko and Zoran Vujović became the second pair of twins to play in the World Cup finals but the team did not make it past the first round.

Perhaps the most famous brothers to grace the World Cup stage were Cameroonians François Omam-Biyik and André Kana-Biyik in 1990, albeit for very different reasons. The Biyik boys certainly made an immediate impression in their first match against the holders Argentina. François headed the only goal of the game while Andre showed the uglier side of the Indomitable Lions by almost cutting Claudio Caniggia in half and being rightly sent off just after the hour mark. Cameroon held on for a famous victory despite being reduced to nine men following the dismissal of Benjamin Massing late on.

In 1998 the Laudrup brothers, Michael and Brian, shone in the Danish team which reached the quarter-finals for the first time in their history, where they narrowly lost 3-2 to Brazil. Another pair of brothers from Scandinavia did manage to mastermind the defeat of Brazil in France when Tore André and Jostein Flo combined to good effect in the surprise result of the first round. For good measure their cousin Håvard also played, so the Norwegians could be said to have very much gone with the Flo.

BITS 'N' BOBS AND BALLS

Uruguay's delayed introduction to the fray and the opening of the Estadio Centenario came a few days later than originally planned as they took on Peru and a crowd of more than 57,000 were relieved to see the hosts squeeze home courtesy of a goal from Héctor Castro. Castro can claim to be the only one-armed player to score in the World Cup finals as he had lost the lower part of his left arm in a carpentry accident when he was 13 years old. Castro also scored the fourth goal when Uruguay beat their old adversary, Argentina in the final.

In recent times there has been much lively debate and a fair amount of hot air expelled over the issue of the balls used in the World Cup finals and the tone for so much of this was set in the 1930 final. After neither side would agree to use a ball made by their opponents, a compromise was reached whereby the Argentinian-made ball would be used in the first half and then replaced by the Uruguayan one after half-time.

The fact that the Argentinians were 2-1 ahead after 45 minutes when using their ball, only for Uruguay to score three unanswered goals after the switch to their version does strongly imply that there was some rationale in their preference for using their own balls. There have been suggestions that this was the origin of the tired old aphorism 'a game of two halves', which makes sense even though it may well be apocryphal.

CONTINENTAL DRIFT

The 1930 tournament was the only one where European countries would be outnumbered, with just four out of the 13 entrants. As the next two tournaments were played in Italy and France the majority of competing nations understandably came from Europe. By the time the World Cup was staged in South America again in 1950, the growth of commercial air travel made crossing the Atlantic a far easier and more affordable option, so there was an even balance between the number of South/Central American and European countries.

By winning the 1930 World Cup Uruguay started the pattern of the dominance of continental winners, which has continued up to the present day. And so Brazil are the only South American country to win in Europe when they triumphed in Sweden in 1958 while Germany returned the favour by winning in Brazil in 2014, becoming the only European country to win any of the eight World Cups that have been hosted in the Americas. Uruguay's win on home soil also set the precedent for domestic dominance with the home country prevailing in a third of the next 15 competitions. Italy in 1934, England in 1966, West Germany in 1974, Argentina in 1978 and France in 1998 all following suit.

PLAYERS - GOALSCORERS

Considering the general disinterest of the United States in the sport, with apparently not one reporter covering their first match in Montevideo against Belgium, it was with some irony that the first player to score a hat-trick was an American. Bert Patenaude achieved the feat in the USA's second match, the 3-0 defeat of Paraguay, although this wouldn't be officially acknowledged for nearly 70 years.

FIFA originally credited the second goal to Patenaude's team-mate, Tom Florie, while others listed it as an own goal. Clearly there was little or no support from the American press as they had not bothered to cover their team's progress and the absence of any televised evidence added a further layer of obfuscation. For seven decades the doubts cast over Patenaude's hat-trick meant that Argentine Guillermo Stábile was considered to be the scorer of the first World Cup hat-trick as he had notched three goals a few days after Patenaude.

Even by the fairly pedestrian and arcane standards of football authorities, and in particular FIFA, the resolution was a long time coming. Amazingly it was not until 2006 that the issue was finally settled when FIFA acknowledged the legitimacy of Patenaude's treble. It took over a decade's lobbying by Colin Jose, an American football historian, to provide the evidence to confirm the hat-trick. Jose took up Patenaude's case in the 1990s as he started to conduct his own research among surviving members of the team. Unfortunately Patenaude was not around to enjoy the official affirmation of his achievement, as he died in 1974, aged 65 but at least he is now in the record books for perpetuity.

Stábile did have the consolation of being the top scorer in the tournament with eight goals but his route to getting there was anything but conventional. Stabile did not feature in the Argentinians' first game against France as Manuel Ferreira, the captain, naturally started. But Ferreira's availability for the second group game was compromised not by injury or suspension but by the fact that he was due to take a law exam and so Stábile deputised. Stábile took this opportunity and how. He scored a hat-trick in his first game against Mexico and although Ferreira returned after finishing his scholarly duties, Stábile was understandably kept in the team as he continued his rich vein of scoring form. In the last group game he scored two and followed that up with another double in the semi-finals. He rounded things off with a goal in the final thus scoring in each of the four games he played in. Not bad for a replacement.

Other players also secured permanent places in the record books, albeit for less admirable reasons than Patenaude. Plácido Galindo of Peru became the first player to be sent off in the World Cup finals while Mexico's Manuel Rosas added being the scorer of the first own goal to being one of the first brothers to appear. Considering the microscopic attention that is now focused on refereeing decisions, Gilberto de Almeida Rêgo the man in the middle for Argentina's group game against France match would have copped a considerable amount of flak as he ended the match six minutes before the end. The French had been on the verge of scoring an equaliser and after an almighty kerfuffle the game was re-started and the closing minutes were duly played out, goalless.

FOOTNOTE

With a population of just under two million in 1930 Uruguay has been by some distance the smallest country to both have hosted the World Cup and also to have won it. The next smallest host is Switzerland with almost double the population while the next smallest winner is England, with over 50 million more people.

1934

HOST
Italy

CITIES
Rome, Milan, Naples, Florence,
Genoa, Bologna, Turin, Trieste

DEBUTANTS (10)
Austria, Czechoslovakia, Egypt,
Germany, Hungary, Italy, Netherlands,
Spain, Sweden, Switzerland

FINAL
Sunday 10 June, Nazionale del DNF,
Rome (50,000)

ITALY (0) (1) 2
Orsi, Schiavio

V

CZECHOSLOVAKIA (0) (1) 1
Puc
(Half-time, full time score in brackets)

TOTAL ATTENDANCE
362,984 over 17 matches (Average 21,352)

TOP GOALSCORER (5)
Oldřich Nejedlý, Czechoslovakia

"THE HOME NATIONS [TOURNAMENT] WAS A FAR MORE REPRESENTATIVE WORLD CHAMPIONSHIP THAN WHAT IS TAKING PLACE IN ROME."

Charles Sutcliffe, FA representative

INTRODUCTION

The refusal by the leading teams to entertain the idea of intercontinental travel became a regular occurrence in the early years of the World Cup, indeed it led to 1934 being the only time the World Cup holders have not defended the trophy. Uruguay took umbrage at the various European countries non-appearance in their 1930 tournament so in a tit-for-tat manoeuvre they did not travel to Italy in 1934, leaving Argentina and Brazil as the only South American contenders who were joined by the USA as the other representatives from the Americas.

The tournament was the first to have some form of pre-qualification process although it was a little half-hearted and a trifle random with even the hosts Italy being asked to play Greece who they dispatched with the minimum of fuss. It is difficult to imagine how the authorities would have reacted if the Italians had not beaten Greece but there would certainly have been a mighty uproar, not least from Mussolini who saw this as an opportunity to show the world how fascism works. One of the more bizarre qualification matches of this or indeed of any World Cup was arranged a few days prior to the staging of the finals when Mexico and USA had to play in Rome. Mexico's consequent departure left a nasty taste in the mouth. Not only had their opponents applied to enter late in the day but having travelled all that way the Mexicans did not even get the chance to compete in the tournament proper. That is a long way to go to fall at the final hurdle.

The end result of all this was that rather than the ungainly and untidy 13 countries from 1930 there were 16 teams, rendering this tournament a straight knock-out system. The entire first round of matches were played simultaneously on 27th May and thus within a couple of hours all those who had travelled from across the Atlantic—Argentina, Brazil and USA—were packing their bags, leaving the quarter-finals as a purely European affair. The Uruguayans were no doubt affording themselves a wry smile at the inconvenience. This was the only time that one continent would so dominate the last eight and the balance between the two most powerful regions with the addition of increasing competition from Asia and Africa has led to greater diversity in the latter stages of the finals.

PLAYERS

One of the most interesting players in this tournament was Luis Monti who had switched allegiance from the beaten finalists Argentina to Italy and who would go on to win the World Cup with his newly adopted country. He was the most notable member of the *oriundi*, a group of players who played for two different countries and were mainly composed of South Americans who took advantage of being of European descent and made the transition from one country to another without any objections from the authorities. Jack Charlton was not the first to think long and hard about genealogy.

Monti was not the only member of that victorious Italian team to have switched nationalities. Enrique Guaita who scored the only goal in their semi-final and Raimondo Orsi, who scored the equaliser against Czechoslovakia in the final, were both Argentinian by birth. Add to those two crucial goals the fact that Monti, the midfield lynchpin who broke up the opposition's attacks before launching the Italians on the counter, was instrumental in manager Vittorio Pozzo's formation and the importance of this trio could not be overestimated. The other fulcrum of Pozzo's team was rampaging inside-forward Giuseppe Meazza who, according to John Foot in *Calcio,* his excellent history of Italian football, "was the most famous player of his generation, a legend, the first Italian footballing superstar". Meazza was given his debut by Pozzo in 1930 and had established himself in the national team by the time the World Cup had moved to Italy. Meazza's opponents were not so enamoured by the 24-year old's over-physical approach. Both Spain and Austria, who lost to Italy in the quarter-finals and semi-finals respectively, complained that Meazza's many fouls went unpunished. This thinly veiled criticism of the referees favouring the hosts would become another well-worn theme throughout World Cup history, rearing its head too often to be dismissed entirely as a fanciful notion.

In the Final between the hosts and Czechoslovakia both teams were captained by their goalkeepers, Giampiero Combi and Frantisek Planicka respectively. This remains the only time that both finalists' captains have been keepers. Combi had announced his intention to stop playing international football but Pozzo coaxed him out of retirement to be the back-up to his first choice keeper Carlo Ceresoli. When Ceresoli was injured just before the World Cup started, Combi not only replaced him but as the most experienced player he was also made captain. Alongside Combi there are only two other goalkeepers who have captained the winning team, his fellow Italian Dino Zoff did so in 1982, when he also became the oldest World Cup winning captain at the age of 40. The third of the triumvirate is Iker Casillas who led the victorious Spanish side in 2010.

FOOTNOTE

Egypt were the first African country to reach the World Cup Finals and they put up a good fight against Hungary, one of the strongest European teams, coming back from being two goals down to equalise before they were eventually seen off 4-2. It would take another 56 years for them to qualify again and coincidentally when they did make it the Italians were yet again the hosts. Egypt's next World Cup Finals will be in Russia in 2018 when ironically the Italians have failed to qualify.

1938

HOST
France

CITIES
Paris, Marseilles, Bordeaux,
Lille, Toulouse, Strasbourg,
Reims, Antibes, Le Havre

DEBUTANTS (4)
Cuba, Dutch East Indies, Norway, Poland

FINAL
Sunday 19 June. Stade Olympique
Yves-du-Manoir, Colombes, Paris (45,000)

ITALY (3) 4
Colaussi 2, Piola 2
V
HUNGARY (1) 2
Titkos, Sárosi
(Half-time score in brackets)

TOTAL ATTENDANCE
375,696 over 18 matches (Average 20,872)

TOP GOALSCORER (7)
Leônidas, Brazil

"UP TO FIVE GOALS IS JOURNALISM. AFTER THAT, IT BECOMES STATISTICS."

Emmanuel Gambardella,
French journalist reporting on Sweden 8 Cuba 0.

INTRODUCTION

The quality of the 1938 tournament was also diminished by the absence of some of the stronger countries for either logistical or political reasons. Both the 1930 finalists, Argentina and Uruguay, refused to take part. The Uruguayans were still justifiably angry at the reluctance of the Europeans to participate in the 1930 tournament. While the Argentinians were also angry as they were snubbed in favour of France to host the finals. There has to be some sympathy for them as FIFA had reneged on an earlier agreement to alternate between continents—this proved to one of only two occasions when the same continent hosted successive tournaments (the other was when Sweden followed Switzerland as hosts in 1958).

The Spanish withdrew before the qualification rounds due to the Civil War. The Austrians did qualify but were denied entry as a separate team just months before the World Cup was due to begin because of the *Anschluss* and, much to their chagrin, their best players were absorbed into the German side. However one player, Matthias Sindelar, who was considered Austria's best player, was adamant that he was not going to play for the Germans.

Sindelar who was known as *The Paper Man* because of his sinewy figure, had had the audacity to not only score against Germany in a match to 'celebrate' the annexation of Austria but also to celebrate wildly in front of the watching Adolf Hitler and his cohorts, who were naturally fuming at such effrontery. Sindelar's mysterious death in his flat a year later has never been fully explained and a cloud of suspicion still hangs over the circumstances. But justice of a kind was served when Germany lost in the first round to Switzerland, which is the only time they have failed to reach the second round.

The original plan was to have 16 teams compete in the tournament and so England were invited to replace the Austrians. But yet again the FA president Sir Stanley Rous declined to participate as the English still deemed the competition not worth entering. At least they did send representatives across the Channel to observe what all the fuss was about, unlike the two previous World Cups that they had blithely ignored. Consequently, Austria's slot remained unfilled and there were just 15 countries left to compete in France. This was the third World Cup and there still had not been a consistent number of teams competing, a fact that illustrated the slightly haphazard nature of the organisation in its formative years and the external forces that made it all the more difficult to arrange.

MINNOWS

Of the four countries that made their bow in 1938 the most interesting was the Dutch East Indies, who were the first Asian nation to appear in the World Cup finals. However, they had the misfortune to come up against Hungary, one of Europe's strongest teams, in the first round and subsequently lost their one and only match 6-0. They did not get the chance to play another game as there were no groups in this World Cup, just a straight knock-out whereas Hungary went on to reach the final. Before the next staging of the World Cup in 1950 the Dutch East Indies ceased to exist. In 1945 Indonesia nationalists declared independence from the Netherlands and since then Indonesia have not come close to emulating their colonial ancestors in qualifying for the finals.

Cuba, the only team that travelled from the Americas other than Brazil, were another country making their debut in the finals. They benefitted from the countries like Mexico joining their South American neighbours in boycotting the finals. Thus Cuba became the first Caribbean nation to play at the World Cup and remarkably they were one of eight seeded teams alongside established nations such as Brazil, France and Italy. Their first round opponents Romania had similarly benefited from the decision of Egypt, who they were due to play in qualifying, to withdraw.

Cuba fared a great deal better than the Dutch East Indies and upset the odds by beating the experienced Romanians, who were one of only four countries alongside Belgium, Brazil and France to be competing in their third successive tournament. In the first game in Toulouse the Cubans fought back a couple of times after being behind, eventually drawing 3-3 after extra time. For the replay the manager took a very bold and some said foolhardy decision to drop the impressive goalkeeper Benito Carvajales for No.2 keeper, Juan Ayra.

Rather than being bitter about being replaced, Carvajales confidently predicted the result, announcing to the press: "Gentlemen, I shall not be playing, but we shall win the replay, that's certain. The Romanian game has no more secrets for us, we shall score twice, they will only score once. Adios, Caballeros." And indeed it was *adios* for the Romanians as Carvajales' bold prediction turned out to be spot on with the Cubans showing similar resilience and resolve to the original game in coming back from being 1-0 down at half time to overcome their European counterparts in what was the most notable victory in their footballing history by a country mile.

Because of the limited number of teams competing, the Cubans happily and somewhat incredibly found themselves in the quarter-finals, something that England would not achieve for another 20 years and the Scots have never managed. There is no record of another confident Carvajales forecast and it was probably just as well. Carvajales was restored as keeper but a third game in the space of a week proved too much for the amateurs and they were no match for a fully rested Swedish side who had been granted a bye because of Austria's late withdrawal. The Swedish pair Harry Andersson and Gustav Wetterström both bagged hat-tricks, as Cuba's one and only appearance ended with a 8-0 drubbing. There have only been three World Cup games that have featured two hat-tricks and amazingly one of the other occasions was just a week beforehand, in the Brazil – Poland match when Leonidas and Ernest Wilimowski did so in Brazil's 6-5 victory. The other time was when Theodor Wagner of Austria and Josef Hugi of Switzerland both notched three in the 1954 quarter-final.

Despite this slightly ignominious exit the Cubans can still point to the fact that they are the only Caribbean country to have progressed beyond the first round. Some seven decades later in 2010, the Cuban forward Juan Tuñas gave his explanation of why things had gone so badly awry against the Swedes. He claimed that they considered themselves favourites before the game but were foiled by the filthy European weather rather than the superior footballing ability of their opponents. "But then something happened that we hadn't bargained for. It rained and the pitch was sodden. We weren't used to conditions like that and we kept slipping over," Tuñas said. It was certainly true that the conditions were not ideal and many of the games were played on mud heaps as opposed to the pristine pitches of today. The most entertaining game of the tournament was played in similarly wet, muddy conditions, which undoubtedly contributed to the glut of goals in the aforementioned double hat-trick match as Brazil beat Poland 6-5 after extra time in the first round.

FOOTNOTE

Italy's Giuseppe Meazza proved himself to be an accomplished finisher with a rare sense of composure when taking a crucial penalty during the semi-final against Brazil. If that was not nerve-wracking enough then Meazza's run-up to the spot kick was hindered further by a problem with his shorts, which were loosening as he approached the ball. Meazza had no thought of stopping, he continued without a hitch, nonchalantly dispatching the penalty with his hand firmly gripping his errant shorts to ensure that there was no embarrassment from either a missed spot kick or a wardrobe malfunction. As Meazza and Giovanni Ferrari were the only members of the 1934 final team to appear in the 1938 final they became the first players to win two World Cups.

As well as those individual achievements, the Italians set quite a few records as a team when they overcame Hungary in the Paris Final. They became the first country to retain the trophy, a feat only Brazil have managed to emulate in the 17 tournaments since, with their consecutive wins in Switzerland in 1958 and Chile in 1962. Vittorio Pozzo led the Italians to both victories and so is the only manager to achieve successive World Cup victories as Vicente Feola who led Brazil to success in 1958 was replaced by Aymoré Moreira for the 1962 tournament. Added to this and because of the hiatus caused by the Second World War the Italians actually were World Cup holders for sixteen years. Furthermore by winning in France they became the first team to win the World Cup outside their own country.

1950

HOST
Brazil

CITIES
Belo Horizonte, Curitiba, Porto Alegre, Recife,
Rio de Janeiro, Sao Paulo

DEBUTANTS (1)
England

FINAL[1]
Sunday 16 July, Maracanã,
Rio de Janeiro (174,000[2])

BRAZIL (0) 1
Friaca

V

URUGUAY (0) 2
Schiaffino, Ghiggia
(Half-time score in brackets)

TOTAL ATTENDANCE
1,045,242 over 22 matches (Average 47,511)

TOP GOALSCORER (8)
Ademir, Brazil

1. This was not strictly a Final but a group match that
decided who would win the World Cup

2. The true attendance figure is almost impossible to verify with some
estimates putting it at over 225,000 with so many people gaining entry
without official admission. The figure quoted is from FIFA.

"I HAVE GOT MANY GREAT WORLD CUP MEMORIES, BUT THE FIRST OF THEM ALL IS BRAZIL LOSING THE WORLD CUP THAT YEAR. IT WAS THE FIRST TIME I EVER SAW MY FATHER CRY, AND ALL BECAUSE OF THAT DEFEAT. I WAS NINE OR TEN YEARS OLD AND I REMEMBER SEEING HIM SITTING NEXT TO THE RADIO, SOBBING."

Pelé

INTRODUCTION

Because of the enforced break brought about by the Second World War a dozen years passed without any World Cup action. By this time England had been accepted back into the fold of FIFA, having rejoined in 1946 and finally after so much procrastination by the FA they made their World Cup debut under the guidance of Walter Winterbottom. Following such a long wait they would live to regret their arrival on the global stage.

HOSTS - CROWDS

Brazil who were due to hold their first World Cup in 1942 were retained as the hosts for the much-delayed staging of the fourth World Cup Finals. The World Cup's return to South America was greeted with unbounded enthusiasm and the Brazilians' insatiable appetite for football was clearly illustrated by the massive crowds that watched all Brazil's games. The aggregate audience for their six games was greater than the total for any of the previous three World Cups and included the four largest World Cup crowds, all greater than 138,000, ever recorded. Like Estadio Centenario 20 years beforehand the Maracanã stadium in Rio was commissioned specifically for the World Cup and just as in 1930 the construction endured many hiccups and delays along the way and it was finally completed with literally days to go before the opening match. Even then the hurried finish to the building left some of the parts of the stadium in disrepair and inadvertently led to Yugoslavia's Rajko Mitic missing the start of the group match against Brazil having hit his head on a stray girder.

It was just as well that the Maracanã was finished at the final hour, as the other five stadia would not have been able to accommodate the vast crowds. For the first time the aggregate attendance for the World Cup finals exceeded the million mark and the appetite for the competition was established. The reported figure for Brazil's crucial last game of the tournament with Uruguay vary somewhat with some suggesting that the crowd was well in excess of the official capacity of 200,000 but even FIFA's more modest figure of 174,000 is by far and way the largest attendance for any football match. The next three largest World Cup crowds ever achieved were Brazil's games at the 1950 tournament against Spain – 152,772, Yugoslavia – 142,429 and Sweden – 138,886. While the next largest World Cup attendance of 114,580 was the 1986 World Cup Final in the Azteca in Mexico City, which is some way behind.

It was abundantly clear that the Brazilian public were thrilled by their chance to host the World Cup but their unrivalled fanaticism was not matched by the enthusiasm of other countries where politics took precedence over football. Even in the post-war era there were still a host of nations who took umbrage and refused to enter the competition, the most notable of which were Brazil's neighbours, Argentina who were still smarting from a variety of wrangles with the Brazilian Federation. Germany were barred and none of the strong Eastern Europeans made the journey. Yet again as a result of a series of withdrawals several countries did not need to qualify, which illustrated that the World Cup was still in its infancy and was not yet an established element of the international football calendar. Also amongst those who withdrew were India. Despite a much-told, but almost certainly apocryphal, tale that the refusal to allow them to play barefoot was the reason behind their withdrawal it seems more likely that the cause was that they could not afford to finance their trip and FIFA were not willing to 'foot' the bill.

ENGLAND'S LATE ARRIVAL & EARLY DEPARTURE

England did have to qualify and the four-team Home Championships were chosen as the conduit. The original agreement was that the top two countries would travel to Brazil but Scotland had declared that they would not go unless they were outright winners. And so when they came second to England and despite entreaties from players and fans alike the Scots dug their heels in and refused to go. Such stubbornness would be laughable now but the Scots were not alone as even France got cold feet and ducked out. This was embarrassing for the French co-founders and especially for the man who just had the trophy named after him in honour of his involvement in initiating the World Cup. Jules Rimet was in Brazil but the French team was not.

So England were left flying the Union Jack. That they failed dismally in their role even with a team boasting the talents of Stan Mortensen, Tom Finney and a certain Alf Ramsey, is beyond dispute as they were infamously beaten by the USA. Maybe those years of enforced isolation had taken their toll and thus Belo Horizonte became a byword for football humiliation, England style.

England's chief persecutor was Joe Gaetjens, a Haitian by birth who spent most of his career in the American Soccer League for the Brookhattan club for whom he scored over 50 goals. Gaetjens scored only one international goal during a handful of appearances for both the USA and Haiti. But that goal defined Gaetjens' career and to a large extent his life. Although the goal itself may have been on the scruffy side as his long-range shot deflected beyond England goalkeeper Bert Williams, it had huge implications as his appositely entitled biography *The Shot Heard Around The World* suggested. The sense of shock was not felt so keenly at the time but has certainly been embellished retrospectively. It had taken England a long time to decide before entering the World Cup but suffice to say it has taken longer for the nation to come to terms with this indignity and some might argue that not only does it still linger but has actually grown recently with each retelling. At least it did serve a purpose as a handy precursor to a litany of failings over the coming decades. After all, forewarned is forearmed.

England were the only team to drop points against the Americans and after defeat to Spain in their final group match they failed to progress to the second round. History seemed to repeat itself when the World Cup returned to Brazil in 2014 as Roy Hodgson's men went out after the first round. In mitigation the 1950 team could point to the curiously lopsided first round groups. The English were in one of two groups with four teams, while the third group had three teams and ridiculously Uruguay were put in a group that paired them with just one other team. That this team was a very weak Bolivia, who Uruguay duly rolled over 8-0, was particularly galling. Such an easy passage may well have contributed to the Uruguayans' second World Cup title as they only had to play four matches in the entire competition, the least of any World Cup winning side.

HOME DISCOMFORT

This was about as far away from a level playing field as one could possibly imagine and thankfully was the last time there was such uneven distribution in the arrangement of the groups. If that first round was unusual then there was also a new and slightly left-field way of organising the second (and final) round which meant that the four first round group winners progressed to another group, all playing each other in a further round-robin pool. This new approach meant this was the only World Cup without a single knock-out match, which on reflection seems bizarre. FIFA were mighty fortunate that the last group match actually materialised into one that had the destiny of the World Cup hinging on it. The game could just as easily have been a dead rubber and a massive anti-climax but that was thankfully avoided.

As the last fixture was between Uruguay and Brazil there was the added frisson of the hosts taking on local rivals and former World Cup winners. That this was a quasi–final mattered not a jot to the Brazilian population who were whipped into a state of frenzy at the prospect of the country being crowned World Cup winners. In the frenetic build-up to the match the Governor of Rio made a speech that did nothing to dampen the over-excited anticipation of the Brazilian fans by hailing the players "who in less than a few hours will be acclaimed champions by millions of your compatriots". No pressure, then. As an exercise in hubris this was up there among the clearest examples. It was not as much expected as demanded that Brazil would lift the trophy as even a draw would have been enough to deliver the trophy to what the home fans considered its rightful place.

When Brazil scored the first goal just after half-time the celebratory mood kicked into gear and the Uruguayans were expected to play their part in the coronation of the *Seleção*. However, Uruguay found an inner strength and no doubt benefitting from the freshness afforded them by their less than rigorous schedule equalised within 20 minutes and then with just over 10 minutes remaining did the unthinkable as Alcides Ghiggia put them ahead.

The shock to the Brazilian system was deep and far-reaching and the coining of the word *Maracanazo* to describe the national tragedy that took place that July day summed up the collective grief. In an attempt to wipe the shock and horror of *Maracanazo* from their collective memories the Brazilians abandoned the traditional white strip that they had worn up to that point. In its place they adopted the yellow and green that is now closely associated with the success of the glamorous national team who have won more World Cups than any other country. The *Maracanazo* did come back to haunt Brazil in 2014 when despite being hosts and strong favourites they lost 7-1 against Germany in the semi-final. So strangely unlike every other World Cup winner, apart from Spain, the Brazilians have never won the trophy on home soil.

RED CARDS & RED FACES

1950 was, along with the 1970 tournament, one of only two World Cups to be completed without a single sending-off. This is less a reflection of the good old days being less aggressive and more to do with the disciplinary code having been tightened up considerably in recent years. In the first ten tournaments between 1930 and 1974 there were 28 dismissals in total, a number matched by red cards shown in the 2006 World Cup alone. The game is now much stricter on all manner of foul play and this has undoubtedly helped reduce some of the more unsavoury behaviour of players and eradicate the types of matches that disfigured some of the tournaments in the 1950s and 1960s, (as will be covered in the following chapters) while at the same time increasing the number of sending-offs.

FOOTNOTE

Ademir was the leading goalscorer but in the wake of the *Maracanazo* he had to suffer a lonely, dispiriting end to a tournament he had previously lit up. He scored eight goals as Brazil were busy trampling over most of their opponents, but yet again the curse of the Golden Boot meant that for the fourth successive time the leading scorer did not finish on the winning side. Ademir was so distraught after the match that he effectively disappeared. "I went to the dressing room like everybody else but as soon as I could I went away in my car and just kept driving I ended up going to Ito Curacao, an island not too far away from Rio de Janeiro, and I just stayed there for 15 days. I phoned Vasco de Gama to tell them where I was but in reality I just had to get away from everybody." It is unlikely that any of the other leading goal scorers spent so much time licking their wounds but such was the sense of despair for all Brazilians and in particular poor old Ademir.

1954

HOST
Switzerland

CITIES
Basel, Berne, Geneva,
Lausanne, Lugano, Zurich

DEBUTANTS (3)
Scotland, South Korea, Turkey

FINAL
Sunday 4 July, Wankdorf Stadium, Berne (60,000)

WEST GERMANY (2) 3
Morlock, Rahn 2
V
HUNGARY (2) 2
Puskás, Czibor
(Half-time score in brackets)

TOTAL ATTENDANCE
768,586 over 26 matches (Average 29,561)

TOP GOALSCORER (11)
Sándor Kocsis, Hungary
(including two hat-tricks)

"I THOUGHT IT WAS GOING TO BE THE GREATEST GAME I WOULD EVER SEE. I WAS ON TOP OF THE WORLD. WHETHER POLITICS OR RELIGION HAD ANYTHING TO DO WITH IT I DON'T KNOW, BUT THEY BEHAVED LIKE ANIMALS. IT WAS A DISGRACE."

Arthur Ellis, the English referee for The Battle of Berne.

INTRODUCTION

After their enforced exile from the previous World Cup West Germany returned to the global stage with some impact, being responsible for one of the largest turnarounds in World Cup history. After being humbled 8-3 in a group match by Hungary the Germans were 2-0 down after just eight minutes of the final and it seemed a second humiliation was about to meted out by the Mighty Magyars, Ferenc Puskás *et al*. The Hungarians, at the time the powerhouse of European football, were on a four year 32-match unbeaten run during which they won the 1952 Olympic tournament. They had also scored a further nine goals in their other World Cup group game, against South Korea, so they were clearly in a rich vein of form. In their five games during the tournament they went on to score 27 goals, averaging over five a game which remains a record tally.

However, the resilience for which the Germans became both envied and renowned, came to the fore when they responded with two quick fire goals of their own. After 19 minutes the scores were level, no other final has matched that sort of electric start. The next highest score after 20 minutes was the 1938 final when the Italians were 2-1 up. Of course the Germans then wrapped things up with five minutes left and their dominance of the international scene was underway. No other team has come back from being two goals down to win a final.

However, rumours soon began to circulate that the Germans' remarkable recovery was less the result of a national trait but more to do with external factors. The sight of syringes in the victors' dressing room fuelled such speculation but the Germans claimed these were just for vitamin injections. Soon after the game had finished several players were taken quite seriously ill and the accusation was levied that they had shared the same needle and were consequently suffering from jaundice. An investigation commissioned by the German authorities and conducted by Leipzig University almost 50 years later revealed that these were not vitamins being injected as was originally claimed but was in fact an amphetamine called Pervitin, nicknamed 'Panzer chocolate', which had been used extensively by troops during the Second World War.

And so Germany's first World Cup triumph was somewhat tarnished as the duopoly of Uruguay and Italy was broken 24 years after that first tournament in Montevideo. Over the 16 World Cups between 1954 and 2014 the Germans would be involved in 43% of the finals, winning three and appearing in another four finals. This was a record even the mighty Brazilians could not equal as they contested six finals over the same period albeit winning five of them. So dominant have these two nations been that there have been only three post-War finals that have not featured either Brazil or Germany, but they have only met once in a final, in 2002.

Germany's route to the Final in Berne was a little convoluted. In their infinite wisdom FIFA changed the way the first round of matches were arranged. The curious make-up of the Group stages led to two seeded teams playing only against the two non-seeded teams, so the four-team group involved just two matches for each team. This rather cack-handed approach led to Germany having to beat Turkey in a play-off when both countries finished level on two points. The Germans won comfortably enough and then went all the way to that victory over Hungary. But it is worth noting that if this had happened in modern times Germany would have been out of the competition because of an inferior goal difference.

WORLD CUP DEBUTANTS

Scotland arrived for their first World Cup. Although they had again finished as runners-up in the Home Nations championship, they graciously decided that they would take up the qualification slot. In retrospect they probably wished they had not bothered as their debut did not yield them a point or even the consolation of a goal and to compound their misery they were hammered 7-0 by the Uruguayans in their last game. So the Scots left their first tournament with their tails firmly tucked between their legs, which was unfortunately to become a depressingly regular occurrence over the coming years.

At least the Scots could claim that there was a worse team than them in the shape of South Korea who suffered two heavy defeats at the hands of Hungary and the third debutant Turkey. The combined aggregate of 0-16 meant that the South Koreans have the indignity of the highest number of goals conceded per match by a World Cup finalist. Turkey benefited from having played the weakest side in World Cup history, which, along with the bizarre seeding procedure, helped them to their unsuccessful play-off encounter with the eventual winners.

Turkey's route to their first ever tournament is a strong candidate for one of the strangest qualifications in history. After they had shared one win apiece with Spain over two legs there was a play-off game in Rome that finished as a 2-2 draw and this was when the fun really began. There are varying reports as to what happened next including the rather bizarre solution of choosing a local youth who was blindfolded in order to draw straws. FIFA officially said that it was all down to the toss of a coin, but whichever method was used it was the Spanish who drew the short straw and Turkey who progressed via the most circuitous of routes to Switzerland.

Having eliminated Spain, who would have been seeded, Turkey gained a considerable advantage by becoming one of the seeded teams and therefore did not have to play Hungary, the other seeded team in their group. Another curious anomaly of how this tournament was organised was that the four Group winners played each other rather than being drawn against second-placed teams so Hungary faced Brazil and England met with Uruguay in the quarter-finals. Suffice to say this was the last time such a lopsided, unfair and quite frankly barmy system was used.

RED CARDS AND RED FACES

"The Battle of Berne" has been well documented and is well-known for the brutal thuggery and malevolent atmosphere that poisoned a match that had provisionally promised so much. Brazil were still recovering from the *Maracanazo* of 1950 but were still a fine, flowing side with talented players such as Julinho and free-kick specialist Didi, and they were expected to be one of the few teams that could hold a candle to the formidable Hungarians. This should have been the epitome of the Beautiful Game but it turned out to be as far away from such lofty expectations as was possible, turning into one of the ugliest games ever played under the auspices of the World Cup.

English referee Arthur Ellis, who had incidentally been a linesman for the deciding match between Uruguay and Brazil in 1950, was looking forward to a classic encounter between the cream of Europe and South America. Instead he was thoroughly shocked by the level of violence and intimidation that unfolded. In the end he congratulated himself on getting the match completed. Ellis even had to link arms with two players Jozsef Bozsik of Hungary and Nilton Santos of Brazil to ensure they left the pitch after they were sent off for exchanging blows in the second half.

The trouble continued unabated for the rest of the game after the Bozsik-Santos clash and although only one more player was dismissed, Brazilian Humberto Tozzi, there could have been a handful more as the majority of the players sought to resolve their personal battles through physical retribution. Ellis later commented on his regret over how the game unfolded. "It was a horrible match," he said. "In today's climate so many players would have been sent off and the game would have been abandoned. My only thought was that I was determined to finish it." The Brazilians were not so impressed by Ellis' officiating and even raised a formal complaint, suggesting that the referee was all part of a communist plot to aid Hungary.

But the final whistle was by no means the end of the hostilities, in fact it was a signal for an escalation of violence as bottles were thrown along with the odd punch. The Hungarian coach Gusztáv Sebes was reportedly struck by one of those bottles and had to have several stitches for a facial wound. The Brazilians took out their frustration by storming the Hungarian dressing room to confront their adversaries in the chaotic post-match scenes. Sebes' description of the free-for-all summed up how matters got worse off the pitch. "Players clashed in the tunnel and a small war broke out in the corridor to the dressing rooms—everyone was having a go; fans, players and officials."

Amazingly, there were was no action taken by FIFA who effectively washed their hands of the affair by giving the responsibility of punishment to the respective federations which inevitably led to nothing being done. Even Puskás was cited as being one of the main transgressors in the turbulent aftermath and he admitted in his autobiography that he had forcibly dragged one of the Brazilian players into the dressing room but released him before too much damage was done.

MEDIA

Unfortunately for FIFA all the terrible events at the Wankdorf stadium were caught on camera as this was the first World Cup to feature live television coverage of matches. Mind you the breadth and depth of that coverage was pretty minimal and nothing like what we are accustomed to today. The European broadcaster, Eurovision, was in control of the scheduling and would not transmit games simultaneously thus the English television audience were shown the Hungarians 8-3 victory over Germany rather than England's decisive group victory over Switzerland.

For the majority of the games, including England's quarter-final defeat to Uruguay, only the second half was shown live with the first half only warranting cursory highlights a few days later. Even one of the semi-finals was deemed surplus to requirements, with an Agricultural Parade live from Copenhagen considered to be more to the liking of the European audience. So the television revolution started with a whimper rather than a bang and it would not be until the 1970 World Cup that anything approaching blanket coverage would really begin.

FOOTNOTE: GOALS, GOALS, GOALS

This was the World Cup where it rained goals—a scarcely credible total of 140 over just 26 matches which averages at an extremely generous 5.4 per game. To put that into perspective in the 2010 World Cup when there were 64 games, more than twice the number played in 1954, only five more goals were scored, at an average of 2.3. 1970 was the last World Cup in which there was an average of more than three goals per game. If the goals per game average achieved in 1954 was replicated in 2018, there would be over 340 goals scored.

The tournament also featured the highest-scoring match to date when Austria overcame the hosts 7-5, having been 4-2 down at half-time. Amidst this avalanche of goals Sándor Kocsis was the leading individual scorer with 11 and he also became the first player to score two hat-tricks at the finals as he helped himself to seven during the Hungarians' two Group games against South Korea and West Germany. In West Germany's emphatic semi-final triumph over Austria, Fritz and Ottmar Walter became the only brothers to score in the same match at the World Cup Finals and as if to make doubly sure they both scored twice.

1958

HOST
Sweden

CITIES
Boras, Eskilstuna, Gothenburg,
Halmstad, Helsinborg, Malmo,
Norrkoping, Orebro, Sandviken, Solna
(Stockholm), Uddevalla, Vasteras

DEBUTANTS (3)
Northern Ireland, Soviet Union, Wales

FINAL
Sunday 29 June, Rasunda Stadium, Stockholm (51,800)

BRAZIL (2) 5
Vavá 2, Pelé 2, Zagallo

V

SWEDEN (1) 2
Liedholm, Simonsson
(Half-time score in brackets)

TOTAL ATTENDANCE
819,810 over 35 matches (Average 23,423)

TOP GOALSCORER (13)
Just Fontaine, France
(The existing record)

"AFTER THE FIFTH GOAL I DIDN'T WANT TO MARK PELÉ ANY MORE. I JUST WANTED TO APPLAUD HIM."

Sigge Parling, Swedish defender

INTRODUCTION

Sweden followed Switzerland as European hosts, the second and last time the World Cup was staged on the same continent in consecutive tournaments. After the shenanigans of the random group organisation in 1954, thankfully the simplicity of four groups of four teams playing each other in a round-robin format returned and natural order was restored. However, goal difference was still not being used to separate teams finishing on the same number of points, leading to three of the four groups going to play-offs to determine who would qualify for the quarter-finals.

The strong British contingent which saw all four home nations present in Sweden (the only time this has happened), was exemplified by the English league having the highest number of players represented at the finals with 55 in total, and when the Scottish and Welsh were added, almost a quarter of the players were from the British leagues. The British were even allocated their own pot for seeding purposes. Therefore it was no great surprise that all three of the group play-offs games featured British sides. There was a turn up for the books however when the one home nation of the three that failed to capitalise on their second chance were England who were disappointingly beaten by the debutant Soviets. England did at least achieve a record in their group game with Brazil as remarkably, after 109 World Cup matches, this was the first goalless draw. Fellow debutants Wales and Northern Ireland also upset the odds by overcoming their supposed East European superiors Hungary and Czechoslovakia respectively.

One of the main reasons for England's failure was that their squad had been weakened by the loss of several key players, such as Duncan Edwards and Tommy Taylor, who were killed in the Munich Air disaster in February. The psychological impact was equally apparent as illustrated by the 20 year-old Bobby Charlton who was understandably still struggling to come to terms with the terrible events of a few months earlier and did not play any part in the tournament. One of the other survivors from the crash Northern Irish keeper, Harry Gregg did feature and was instrumental in their impressive progress in the tournament.

DEBUTANTS

Remarkably the three countries that were new to the World Cup finals all made it to the quarter-finals and all three did so via the play-offs. The Soviet Union were reigning Olympic champions and they had predictably topped their qualifying group. Having been held back from participating in previous World Cups for a variety of reasons, their strength proved too much for the weakened English in their play-off.

In qualifying for Sweden, Northern Ireland had surprisingly disposed of the double World Cup winners Italy, although it turned out to be a tempestuous campaign. After they had lost 1-0 in Italy their home leg in Belfast was postponed because bad weather prevented the referee from making it to Windsor Park. The so-called friendly that took its place was only such in name and led to some controversial scenes at the end when the fans invaded the pitch and confronted several of the Italian players, who had not held back in their physical approach to the game.

When the second leg was finally played a month later, it was done so in a pretty rancorous atmosphere. However, Northern Ireland overcame their first leg deficit to emerge victorious as the Italians cowed under the considerable pressure exerted by a passionate home crowd. Until 2018 this was the only World Cup for which Italy had failed to qualify.

Wales' qualification for Sweden was yet another example of political expediency at work rather than supremacy on the pitch. Having finished second to Czechoslovakia in their qualification group they found their way back into the reckoning when several countries refused to play against Israel in a play-off. The Welsh had no such reservations and seized the chance by beating the Israelis home and away, thus securing their passage to their first World Cup.

In their play-off games at the finals, Northern Ireland overcame the Czechs in extra time courtesy of two goals from their top scorer Peter McParland who racked up five goals altogether. But with only two days before the quarter-final there was precious little time to recover. Perhaps the biggest shock of the tournament came in the other play-off where Wales were paired with the Magyars, who although not as mighty as they had been in 1954 but were still expected to account for Wales. The Welsh, led by the inimitable John Charles and bolstered by the solid keeping of Jack Kelsey, were made of sterner stuff than many gave them credit for. They bounced back from being a goal down at half-time to run out worthy 2-1 winners.

All three debutants fell at the next hurdle, the Soviets succumbed to the hosts, Sweden; a weary Northern Ireland were no match for the free-scoring France; an obdurate Wales made life difficult for the eventual champions Brazil until Pelé's first World Cup goal separated the two sides. Pelé had announced his arrival on the world stage and after becoming the youngest player to appear in a World Cup finals. Coincidentally, it was a Northern Irishman who would break his record when Norman Whiteside appeared in 1982 Finals aged 17 years and 41 days. Pelé went on to also become the youngest to score in a final as well as being the youngest World Cup winner. He would add two more World Cup victories to his tally and those last two records still stand today. For Wales, it was to be a fleeting moment of glory as they still await their second World Cup finals.

GOALS – LUCKY 13 & BORROWED BOOTS

Almost 30 years after Lucien Laurent became the first goal scorer in World Cup history another Frenchman made his mark with his goal scoring achievements.

Just Fontaine may never have got the chance to etch his name into the record books as the player to score the most goals in a single World Cup tournament, had it not been for an injury to a colleague. Fontaine was originally not included in the French first team and was given the squad number 17 as he was behind fellow Stade de Reims forward René Bliard in the pecking order. But the Moroccan-born Fontaine was thrust into the limelight once Bliard suffered an injury just before the tournament started and was forced to withdraw.

The 24 year-old grasped the opportunity with some aplomb, scoring a hat-trick in the first game against Paraguay and then adding ten more in the subsequent five matches. His goal scoring prowess was aided by the astute probing of Raymond Kopa, with whom he built an almost telepathic understanding. "He was the striker who best suited my style of play," Kopa said. "He knew exactly what I was doing and I could be sure of finding him at the end of one of my dribbles."

Fontaine achieved all this with a pair of boots borrowed from squad player Stéphane Bruey after his own were damaged, making it all the more noteworthy. As Fontaine explained, resources were rather limited, "We just had two boots at the time and no sponsor." FIFA had yet to introduce the Golden Boot award, so to commemorate his achievements, a Swedish newspaper enterprisingly presented Fontaine with the rather surreal prize of an air rifle, no doubt this was chosen as he was such a deadly shooter.

Some might gripe about the circumstances being much kinder to strikers in those days but Fontaine himself scoffs at such a suggestion pointing to the much heavier ball that was less prone to swerving, the logistics of cumbersome travel arrangements and the unprofessional nature of the support services. "The last great World Cup scorer, Ronaldo, played against teams such as China and Costa Rica," he said. "Above all else, referees protect strikers much more than they did in my day. So let me repeat: 13 goals is an enormous total. Beating my record? I don't think it can ever be done."

Fontaine never had another opportunity to emulate his feat. Just as injury presented him with his chance in 1958, so injury deprived him of any repeat, curtailing his career and forcing him to retire from international football at the age of 27.

MIND GAMES

Whereas today World Cup squads are routinely accompanied by psychologists, Brazil's decision to take one to Sweden was considered pretty radical. Dr Joao Carvalhes was appointed partly to try and erase the memory of the *Maracano* and some argued that he had an undue influence over team selection, even though he knew little about football. His insistence on all the players drawing pictures of people, which were then analysed for their psychological profile, led to both Pelé and Garrincha being left out of the side for the first two group matches. Carvalhes' assessment of Pelé was especially caustic and erroneous. "Pelé is obviously infantile. He lacks the necessary fighting spirit." Fortunately for Brazil, the manager Vicente Feola was not swayed and eventually picked both players for the last group game against Russia and for all the knock-out games. This represented a triumph for football sense winning out over mind games.

The influence of Carvalhes foreshadowed the work of Regina Brandão in the 2014 finals and in particular the disastrous semi-final against Germany, which alongside the *Maracanazo* represents the worst football experience in the nation's psyche. Brandão used similar method to Carvalhes with players given various pictures of human faces, ranging from shiny, happy people to those sporting grimaces and their responses were then analysed in an attempt to put them at ease before the game. That this backfired is an understatement. Such a spectacular fall from grace could not have been anticipated, even by the most perceptive of psychologists.

FOOTNOTE

As a precocious, supremely talented teenager who scored six goals in the quarter-final, semi-final and final, Pelé rightly grabbed all the headlines in 1958. However, there was another player in the final who also broke a record, this one was at the other end of the age spectrum, although he very much slipped under the radar of the general public. This was the man who actually opened the scoring in the final giving Sweden the lead—the only time in the whole tournament that Brazil were behind albeit for only five minutes before the Brazilians took hold of the game courtesy of their 17-year-old tyro. That man was Nils Liedholm and as it was a goal that Pelé himself described as the best he had ever seen scored against Brazil it clearly deserved more recognition. At the grand old age of 35 years 263 days, Liedholm became the oldest scorer in a World Cup final before his illustrious counterpart, who was half his age, made his mark.

Liedholm was the Swedish captain that day and was one of several Swedish players who moved to Italy for their club football, spending over 10 years at AC Milan and captaining them in their 1958 European Cup Final defeat to Real Madrid. Liedholm's outstanding fitness was a contributory factor to his longevity as he undertook additional athletics training including running at various distances, plus the javelin and even the shot put twice a week. From his efforts in the athletics field he developed a long throw-in that could propel the ball into the penalty area from the halfway line—the 1950s Rory Delap perhaps.

'The Baron', as Liedholm was affectionately known in Italy, did go on to achieve something which Pelé never did as he not only became a success whilst playing in one of the most powerful European leagues but he also forged an extremely impressive managerial career with Roma as well as AC Milan. So although he was overshadowed that afternoon in Stockholm he did make up for it during the remainder of his career, creating his own legendary status amongst the *cognoscenti* of Italian football.

1962

HOST
Chile

CITIES
Arica, Rancagua, Santiago, Vina del Mar

DEBUTANTS (2)
Bulgaria, Colombia

FINAL
Sunday 17 June, Nacional Stadium, Santiago (69,000)

BRAZIL (1) 3
Amarildo, Zito, Vavá
V
CZECHOSLOVAKIA (1) 1
Masopust
(Half-time score in brackets)

TOTAL ATTENDANCE
893,152 over 32 matches (Average 27,911)

TOP GOALSCORERS (4 GOALS EACH)
Flórián Albert, Hungary
Garrincha, Brazil
Valenton Ivanov, USSR
Dražan Jerković, Yugoslavia
Leonel Sánchez, Chile
Vavá, Brazil

"THE GAME YOU ARE ABOUT TO SEE IS THE MOST STUPID, APPALLING, DISGUSTING AND DISGRACEFUL EXHIBITION OF FOOTBALL POSSIBLY IN THE HISTORY OF THE GAME. CHILE VERSUS ITALY, THIS IS THE FIRST TIME THE TWO COUNTRIES HAVE MET AND WE HOPE IT WILL BE THE LAST."

David Coleman, BBC commentator on 'The Battle of Santiago'.

INTRODUCTION

The 1962 tournament was characterised by some of the most brutal, most violent football imaginable. The beauty of the game was buried behind a particularly dirty cloud and it seems entirely appropriate that no one was able to net more than four goals and that this was the only time the top-scorer accolade was shared between six players. Brazil just about managed to rise above the deeply unsavoury atmosphere and became the second country to successfully defend their title, following in the wake of the Italians' wins in 1934 and 1938, a feat not matched since. But even the *Seleção* were not above the 'dark arts' as had been witnessed in their encounter with Hungary back in 1954.

In the absence of Pelé, who was injured in their second group game against Czechoslovakia, it was their best player Garrincha who decided to take matters into his own hands. Garrincha had been in irresistible, sparkling form in the quarter-final victory against England and his two goals were just reward for his match-winning performance. In the semi-final against the hosts Chile, Garrincha was again at the fore with his unusual brand of trickery and he added another couple of goals to his brace in the previous match. Chile's main tactic to subdue the Brazilian was to instruct Eladio Rojas to kick lumps out of him at regular intervals.

Garrincha eventually got fed up with the rough treatment from Rojas, retaliated and was sent off.

In normal circumstances Garrincha would have missed the next game, which was the final, but this World Cup was not only known for the harsh treatment meted out but also the soft, *laissez faire* attitude of the disciplinary committee. A few days after this game they were somehow persuaded to rescind Garrincha's sending-off, which cleared his path to another final appearance. Rules may be rules but they can clearly be adapted depending on who is going to be affected, or not, as the case may be. Allowing Garrincha to play meant that Brazil had picked exactly the same side for the last four fixtures and throughout the entire tournament they selected only 12 players in their original line-ups. The only change was when Amarildo replaced Pelé after he was injured in their second group game with Czechoslovakia.

The devastating Valdivia earthquake that hit Chile in 1960 and claimed over 50,000 lives not only decimated the infrastructure of the impoverished hosts but also influenced the attitude of many of the visiting teams. The Italian press in particular made many disparaging remarks about Chile and its perceived backwardness, an unwise action that went some way to creating the hostile atmosphere in which the Battle of Santiago took place. In the build up to the game two of the most vocal and dismissive of the journalists, Antonio Ghirelli and Corrado Pizzinelli of *La Nazione* and *Corriere della Sera* respectively, painted a picture of a country plagued by low morals and lacking the fundamental resources necessary to stage a World Cup. The pair had to go into hiding for fear of reprisals and left the country soon afterwards.

Such inflammatory comments would have enraged the mildest citizen and so the scene was set for the match between the hosts and their impertinent guests on 2nd June, a game for which the 1962 World Cup is most remembered. Just like the Battle of Berne it pitted Europeans against South Americans and also it had an Englishman in the middle attempting to exert some sort of control. Ken Aston was the man who had the dubious privilege of refereeing the game and it would unfortunately be the defining moment of his career. Aston replaced the Spanish referee originally appointed as the Italians complained about potential bias, not the last time the Italians would make such an accusation. Aston would much rather be remembered for his initiative to introduce yellow and red cards, which were brought into the World Cup in 1970. If the idea had been in place in 1962 he would have been lost in a blur of colours.

The biggest problem Aston faced was that after the first sending-off of Giorgio Ferrini, which was fully justified as he had kicked Chilean player Honorino Landa with malice aforethought, the Italian refused to leave the pitch. The Italian bench swarmed on to the pitch to protest and the impasse lasted for a full 10 minutes before armed Chilean police intervened to force the player off the pitch and frogmarch him down the tunnel. All these events took place just 12 minutes after kick off. The rest of the match teetered on the brink of anarchy as fights broke out after nearly every malicious tackle, of which there were plenty. Having had his authority undermined by the intervention of the police, Aston was literally and metaphorically fighting a losing battle.

When Chile's Leonel Sánchez escaped any punishment for knocking Mario David to the floor any semblance of order had disappeared. David took his revenge by executing a head-high kick which would not have looked out of place in a martial arts bout and came close to causing serious damage to Sánchez's face. The Italian was sent off, prompting further protests. As the mayhem continued unchecked the police entered the field of play a couple more times, Aston later reflected on his role with just a whiff of exaggeration: "I wasn't reffing a football match, I was acting as an umpire in military manoeuvres."

This infamous game was not an isolated one as the tournament itself quickly descended into a series of the most brutal matches. The undercurrent of violence was never too far from the surface and many of the games were littered with fouls. It seemed that any pent-up hostilities between the various countries were being unleashed. In most World Cups, the early stages are played with some element of caution as teams feel their way into the tournament so more often than not the opening games are tame encounters. There was no such soft acclimatisation in Chile with the first eight games giving a hint of what was to follow with four dismissals, three broken legs and multiple physical and mental scars from the variety of assaults committed.

Just like Ellis four years beforehand, Aston felt that his main achievement was to get to the 90-minute mark. "I expected a difficult match, but not an impossible one," Aston said. "I just had to do the best I could. It did cross my mind to abandon the match, but I could not be responsible for the safety of the Italian players if I did. I thought that then and I still think it now. I tell you one thing: I didn't add on any stoppage time." The outrage felt by the media and anyone who had the misfortune to witness the unseemly goings-on was not reflected in the response from the authorities.

In light of these events a meeting was held between FIFA president, Sir Stanley Rous and a delegation of referees who were understandably concerned about the unruly behaviour. Although FIFA assured the officials that action would be taken, the end result was minimal at best. Ferrini was suspended for a single game whereas incredibly David and Sánchez received reprimands and no suspension. Such a mild rap across the knuckles did not serve the game well and the aggressive behaviour would continue pretty much unchecked into the next World Cup. The tally of six sendings-off for all 32 matches in Chile was the most of the first dozen World Cups but in the circumstances it was paltry as there could have been six in the Chile vs Italy game alone. Such leniency was an indication of weakness from the authorities and not a true reflection of the levels of violence being perpetrated on the pitch.

Although this wretched match was the last World Cup game Aston would referee it was not the end of his brush with refereeing controversy. After Chile he was effectively moved upstairs and was put in charge of the refereeing in England for 1966 finals when there were further acts of indiscipline and more targeting of skilful players such as Pelé to nullify their influence. Yet again a player refused to leave the pitch after being sent off and this incident inspired an innovation in match officiating from Aston that is now an established part of the game, but more of that in the next chapter.

MAD DOGS AND ENGLISHMEN

England's fourth World Cup foray at least saw them qualify for the quarter-finals, having finishing second to Hungary in their Group. But just like 1954 they unfortunately drew South American opponents and this time it was Brazil and so that is where the story ended for Walter Winterbottom's men. The eventual champions eased through by 3-1 and neither of the more vaunted English forwards, Johnny Haynes or Jimmy Greaves, managed to make any real impression on the Brazilian defence.

The pain of that quarter-final defeat was slightly assuaged by Greaves' encounter with a stray dog which at least provided some light entertainment and an opportunity for countless after-dinner speeches. During the first half the dog entered the field of play and managed to evade attempts to catch him by English keeper Ron Springett and Brazilian winger Garrincha. Then Greaves took control of the situation as he recalled: "I got down on my hands and knees, being a dog lover anyway, and called the dog over. It got a massive cheer and I picked the dog up and cuddled him and as I cuddled him he peed all down my shirt. And you never changed strips in those days, you just had the one shirt, so I had to play in this shirt."

Garrincha was so taken by the dog that he adopted it and took it home with him and Greaves claimed he is now known as Garrincha's dog catcher in Brazil. The prolific Greaves may have only scored once for England in the World Cup finals but at least he has been left with an original moniker and is guaranteed instant recognition in Rio.

FOOTNOTE

Incredibly two of the main combatants in the Battle of Santiago later became good friends. Leonel Sánchez and Mario David spent most of the game concentrating on acts of retribution against each other and the continuous fighting only stopped once David had been sent off for his head-high assault on Sánchez. Subsequently they met to patch up their differences having been at each other's throats (literally in David's case after his attack on Sánchez) during the game. In an extraordinary moment of reconciliation that preceded the equally odd Harold Schumacher/Patrick Battiston friendship from 1982, Sánchez and David became firm friends in the aftermath of the battle of Santiago.

1966

HOST
England

CITIES
Birmingham, Liverpool, London, Manchester, Middlesbrough, Sheffield, Sunderland

DEBUTANTS (2)
North Korea, Portugal

FINAL
Saturday 30 July, Wembley Stadium (93,000)

ENGLAND (1) 4
Hurst 3, Peters

V

WEST GERMANY (1) 2
Haller, Weber
(2-2 after 90 minutes, result after extra time)

TOTAL ATTENDANCE
1,563,104 over 32 matches (Average 48,847)

TOP GOALSCORER (9)
Eusebio, Portugal

"I SAW THAT ALL HIS DECISIONS FAVOURED ENGLAND... CORNERS, FOULS, HE EVEN INVENTED HANDBALLS. IN VIEW OF THAT, I SHOWED HIM MY CAPTAIN'S ARMBAND AND FOR SEVERAL MINUTES ASKED FOR AN INTERPRETER TO ASK FOR EXPLANATIONS."

Antonio Rattin, Argentine captain on referee Rudolf Kreitlein.

INTRODUCTION

After England triumphed in a thrilling, high-scoring match against one of their keenest rivals to become champions, Kenneth Wolstenholme predicted that "those lucky enough to see this game will talk about it for years." But Wolstenholme could not have been more mistaken as this match was pretty much forgotten within the space of just a few months. The game in question was the decisive match in the Home Internationals against Scotland at Hampden Park, which took place in April 1966 with England securing the title by winning 4-3.

Naturally the events of 30th July swept away the memories of that earlier English victory. That game is etched into every English football fan's psyche but how many realise that it has a place in the record books as the latest date for a World Cup Final to be held, shared with the original final back in 1930, a game that coincidentally also finished 4-2 to the hosts. As Qatar 2022 is destined to be the first World Cup to take place in the latter months of the year this will record will be ominously broken. The tournaments in Uruguay and England are also the only World Cups to have started in July, rather than June or May. To complete the circle England's opening game in 1966 was an uninspiring, goalless draw against whom else but Uruguay.

Notable omissions from the only World Cup to have been hosted on the British Isles were any of the other Home Nations who all failed to qualify. Scotland would have to wait until 1967 to gain their revenge against the Auld Enemy. Added to the lack of British participants there were no African countries either. They boycotted the tournament because of a perceived bias of offering only a single qualification place for Africa and Asia combined. What really irked them was the uneven distribution that led to Europe being granted 10 of the 16 places up for grabs. This was the last occasion that Africa and Asia would be treated with such high-handedness as from 1970 both continents, which represent 75% of the world's population, were at least guaranteed a minimum of one qualification slot.

The barely concealed disdain expressed by Ghana's Director of Sport and FIFA representative Ohene Djan was encapsulated in his telegram to the world governing body: "Registering strong objection to unfair World Cup arrangement for Afro-Asian countries. Afro-Asian countries struggling through painful expensive qualifying series for ultimate one finalist representation is pathetic and unsound STOP. At the worst, Africa should have one finalist. STOP Urgent—reconsider." The irony of the African boycott coinciding with the only occasion when the leading scorer—Eusebio—was born in Africa would not have been lost on Djan and may even have pricked the conscience of FIFA.

DEBUTANTS

This flawed process did have one happy consequence as it led to the qualification of North Korea, who ended up in a straight showdown with Australia, which they won with room to spare. However, politics threatened to derail their arrival in England as at one stage the British government were contemplating denying the Koreans any entry visas. There was also plenty of diplomatic manoeuvring over the displaying of the North Korean flag and the playing of their national anthem. Eventually there was a fudged compromise that led to no anthems being played apart from in the first game of the tournament and the final.

The North Koreans' 1-0 victory over Italy at Ayresome

Park remains one of the greatest shocks in World Cup history with goalscorer Pak Doo-Ik establishing himself as a legend. It remains by some distance North Korea's most impressive sporting triumph and the team have become part of World Cup folklore. By contrast the vanquished Italians were met by a barrage of rotten tomatoes on their return to Genoa airport following their ignominious exit.

In the quarter-finals the North Koreans met Portugal, the only other debuting country, and gave them an almighty fright when they raced into a staggering 3-0 lead in 25 minutes. Unfortunately for the Koreans the tournament's leading goal scorer Eusebio then took control of proceedings scoring four goals in 32 minutes to haul the Portuguese back into the game and then put them ahead. This burst of scoring remains one of the greatest individual performances in World Cup history.

Aside from the early World Cups, which obviously saw many countries appearing for the first time, Portugal's progress to the semi-finals of the tournament stands out as the greatest achievement by a debutant. The Portuguese were certainly strong finishers as they scored in the last 10 minutes of all six matches they played. That North Korea also reached the quarter-finals far exceeded even the wildest expectations and clearly distinguishes this as the singularly most successful World Cup for debutants.

ANIMALS

After Jimmy Greaves' close encounter with that errant dog in Vina del Mar, there were more canine goings-on in 1966 but on this occasion the dog in question played the role of saviour. Four months before the tournament the FA lent the Jules Rimet trophy in its full gleaming, golden glory to the Stanley Gibbons stamp exhibition at the Methodist Central Hall right in the heart of London. However, the day after the exhibition opened the trophy was stolen.

Two days after the theft a man calling himself Mr Jackson contacted the FA chairman Joe Mears, demanding a £15,000 for the trophy and arrangements were made for an exchange. Mears was told that under no circumstances should he inform the police but he did so. By the time the drop off was set up Mears had fallen ill (he died 12 days before the World Cup kicked off) so the Detective Inspector in charge of the operation, Len Buggy offered to step into his shoes. Buggy was set to rendezvous with Jackson in Battersea Park Jackson's suspicions were aroused and he tried to flee the scene but was apprehended albeit without the trophy. Following his arrest police identified him as Edward Betchley, a 46-year-old petty thief and former soldier. Betchley denied stealing the trophy, claiming to be a go-between rather than the mastermind so the police were no nearer the successful resolution of the crime nor, more significantly, the return of the trophy.

Both the FA and FIFA's English president Sir Stanley Rous grew increasingly exasperated by the continuing absence of the solid gold centrepiece of the tournament. With fears growing that the last had been seen of the priceless item, FA secretary Denis Follows approached silversmith George Bird about creating an exact replica which he duly did in time for the final.

The situation was rescued by a nondescript mixed breed collie called Pickles who unearthed the trophy near to his owner's house in Norwood in South London. The dog's owner David Corbett took it to the police expecting their gratitude, however all he received was a deep-lying suspicion that he was somehow behind the theft. He was soon under interrogation rather than being lauded as someone who had rescued them from an embarrassing situation. Corbett was not best pleased at their insinuations, although he did get his reward when he was asked to the hotel where the players were due to celebrate their victory. Bobby Moore, among others, hoisted Pickles aloft to the crowd assembled outside the team hotel a few hours after he had lifted that trophy at Wembley.

Unfortunately Pickles decided to relieve himself in front of these distinguished guests but at least they avoided Greaves' fate as he did not do so on any of them. Subsequently an agent arranged for Corbett to be handsomely rewarded for taking Pickles on a slew of media appearances as he capitalised on his fifteen minutes of fame. Unfortunately Pickles met an untimely death the following year while on a walk with Corbett's son. He was strangled after his choke chain got caught in a branch. Pickles may have been top dog as far as his discovery was concerned but he was not the only animal to make an impression at the 1966 World Cup. The other was a lion called Willie who was the very first in a long line of faintly ridiculous but instantly recognisable mascots.

RED CARDS AND RED FACES

Animals were also on Sir Alf Ramsey's mind after their quarter-final clash with Argentina as he labelled the South American opposition as such and insisted his players did not swap shirts with their opponents after the match. The tally of fouls committed during the game suggested Ramsey's view was somewhat partial as England were responsible for 33 compared to Argentina's 19. There was only one sending-off but such was the hoo-hah involved it certainly became one of the most infamous. It was another protracted sending-off like the first dismissal in the Chile vs Italy game four years previously. It took ten minutes for Argentina captain Antonio Rattin to leave the pitch after he had been sent off by the German referee Rudolf Kreitlein and in a further echo of Santiago, the police had to get involved to resolve the situation.

Rattin's beef was that he was not quite sure what offence he had committed as there was no outrageous foul or clear indiscretion. He had been booked for a badly-timed challenge on Bobby Charlton and then when he fouled Geoff Hurst he launched into a long and heated debate with the referee, even at one stage asking for an interpreter to clarify the nature of his misdemeanour. Kreitlein's original explanation was not centred on physical violence but rather that of a waspish tongue and he further added rather obliquely that he "did not like the look" on Rattin's face. It was therefore not surprising that the Argentinian questioned the decision with some vigour and even asked for an interpreter to unravel what his offence was. That this was Rattin's only sending-off in his career may dispel the myth that he was a serial troublemaker.

Watching all this unfold was the head of the referees committee, Ken Aston, who had of course seen it all before. The difficulty of removing a player from the pitch would have brought back unhappy memories of his own helplessness in the face of stubborn resistance to accept the referee's decision but his focus was on other matters as he left Wembley that night. Alongside Rattin's dismissal there was further confusion about whether both Charlton brothers had been booked and Aston was toying with how to ensure clarification. Aston drew inspiration on his journey home: "As I drove down Kensington High Street, the traffic light turned red. I thought 'Yellow, take it easy; red, stop, you're off'." By the 1970 World Cup red and yellow cards had been introduced but by a strange quirk of fate that was one of only two tournaments during which there was not one sending-off, the other was in 1950.

FOOTNOTE

Goalless draws are not always the most memorable of games but for Antonio Carbajal the Mexican goalkeeper the 0-0 with Uruguay at Wembley on 19th July represented a high watermark in his remarkable longevity. This was a record fifth successive World Cup for him and after all those games going back to 1950, this was the first time he had kept a clean sheet, something which all goalkeepers cherish. The 37-year-old could retire with an immense sense of pride and satisfaction having finally kept his goal intact. There have been greater keepers of course - Lev Yashin, Gordon Banks and Dino Zoff to name but a few - however, none of them played at five World Cups for which Carvajal will always be remembered.

1970

HOST
Mexico

CITIES
Guadalajara, Leon,
Mexico City, Puebla, Toluca

DEBUTANTS (3)
El Salvador, Israel, Morocco

FINAL
Sunday 21 June, Azteca Stadium, Mexico City (107,412)

BRAZIL (1) 4
Pelé, Gerson, Jairzinho, Carlos Alberto

V

ITALY (1) 1
Boninsegna
(Half-time score in brackets)

TOTAL ATTENDANCE
1,603,968 over 32 games. (Average 50,124)

TOP GOALSCORER (10)
Gerd Müller, West Germany

"BEFORE THE GAME I TOLD MYSELF THAT HE WAS JUST FLESH AND BONES LIKE EVERYBODY ELSE. LATER I REALISED I WAS WRONG."

Tarcisio Burgnich, Italian defender on the
task of man-marking Pelé in the final.

INTRODUCTION

After the bruising encounters that had besmirched the previous few tournaments the World Cup needed to restore its image and thankfully Mexico delivered some of the finest international football. Pelé remained injury-free and proceeded to lead the Brazilian team that is rightly lauded as one of the best, if not the best, to grace the global stage to their third World Cup triumph in four tournaments. Their football was at times utterly mesmerising, never more so than at the business end of the tournament where they amassed 11 goals in their three knockout games, matching West Germany's total from the goal-fest that was Switzerland in 1954 and their own prolific performance in 1958.

Along the way Jairzinho became only the second player to score in every match of a tournament, equalling the achievement of Uruguay's Alcides Ghiggia in 1950. Mind you, Ghiggia only played in four matches whereas Jairzinho did so in six. Added to this, some of Jairzinho's goals were pretty spectacular including his mazy run past three Czech defenders followed by the tidy finish and his thunderous strike against England which was neatly set up by Pelé and decided the tightest of matches.

To make this tournament even more remarkable, as mentioned in the previous chapter, there were no red cards. This was partly due to indulgent refereeing and partly down to a much more free-flowing style of football which saw a reduction in the cynical fouling that had seemed to have become an integral and unwelcome element of the World Cup. This tournament succeeded in lifting the spirits, going a long way to purging the game of previous unpleasantness and reminding everybody of the finer aspects of the "sheer, delightful football" as Kenneth Wolstenhome called it, that we all craved. Fittingly Mário Zagallo, who had won the World Cup as a player with Brazil in 1958 and 1962 became the first man to play in and manage a World Cup winning team as he guided them serenely to their fully deserved victory.

To top it all off there was perhaps the greatest goal ever scored in a World Cup final. The fourth was a liquid move of such sublime skill, exact timing, acute awareness and stylistic elegance that it is hard to see how it could be improved. It had a workmanlike beginning when Tostão tracked back and regained possession, followed by an interchange to Clodoaldo who, with socks rolled down, suddenly injected some pace by embarking on a jinking run that befuddled four Italians who could not get near him. He then slipped the ball to Rivelino on the left-hand touchline who pinged an arcing ball down the line to find Jairzinho, who had significantly switched over from his customary right wing position.

Jairzinho immediately assessed the situation and knew there was now space on the right so he drew two defenders towards him before passing square to Pelé who was positioned some 10 yards outside the area and not being marked tightly. Fully aware of the late run of Carlos Alberto outside him, Pelé did not attempt to go forward himself instead taking a couple of touches before releasing Alberto who by this time was in full flight. The pass was so inviting and perfectly paced it might as well have had a ribbon it, Alberto did not have to break stride as he raced on to the ball ready to unleash his shot. A split second before he shoots the ball took a tiny leap off the pitch into the air that allowed Alberto to turn it into a micro volley.

This small blip could have unsettled lesser mortals but it actually added the final *soupçon* to the perfect dish as the ball was smashed with such authority, sumptuous power and unerring accuracy into the far corner, barely rising more than a foot off the ground. In today's parlance that would have be described as not just a *worldie* but perhaps an 'out-of-this-worldie'. That it was scored by the right back is a testimony to the free-flowing football of that glorious golden team. That it was the Brazilians' captain seems suitably fitting.

As this was Brazil's third triumph they were given the Jules Rimet trophy for good. Well not quite because, as in 1966, the trophy was stolen from the Brazilian FA's Rio headquarters in December 1983 but this time there was no Brazilian Pickles to come to the rescue and a replica was produced and presented to them the following year. The original has never been found. Inevitably, a host of conspiracy theories abound over who stole it and what happened to it. Some Brazilians suggest that it could not have been any of their countrymen as this would be sacrilege for a nation so besotted by football, but was more probably the dastardly work of an Argentinian. Juan Carlos Hernández, a convicted gold dealer, fitted the bill and was convicted along with several others but the trophy was never recovered nor definitive proof of what really happened uncovered, so it remains a tantalising mystery. Even respected writers, such as Simon Kuper, who have tried to discover what really happened have not managed to find the definitive answer and maybe it should remain that way.

DEBUTANTS

The three countries who enjoyed their first tournament were an unusual trio. El Salvador's appearance was more noteworthy because of their short military conflict with Honduras, which had been sparked by a couple of feisty qualifying matches. The two countries won their respective home legs with the away teams being made to feel particularly unwelcome by the opposition fans. A play-off match was held in neutral Mexico City, which El Salvador won 3-2 in extra time. Shortly afterwards Salvadorean troops invaded Honduras triggering the four-day Football War which left about 3,000 soldiers and civilians dead in what was one of the harshest prices ever paid because of a football match.

The El Salvador team did not pull up many trees in their three games, conceding nine without reply and the one moment that most people will remember from their campaign was the lengthy protest of their players when conceding the first goal against the hosts. The Salvadoreans swarmed around the referee, giving him the odd push now and again to press home their grievances. They argued that although they had been given a free-kick, the Mexicans had taken it and duly scored from it as well. The players congregated in the centre circle and made their feelings clear by refusing to restart the match. In an absurd stand-off the referee kept putting the ball on the centre spot only for the players to knock the ball backwards in a show of defiance. This happened numerous times until the last time they did so a player then lumped the ball deliberately into touch and the game could begin again.

Morocco were the first African side to appear in the finals since Egypt in 1934 and they did their continent proud by taking the lead against the Germans and only succumbing to Gerd Müller's late winner (and let's face it there were many teams who could say that they have suffered from Der Bomber's penchant for late, decisive goals, not least England). Despite also losing their next match against the talented Peruvians, Morocco gained a point in their final group game with a 1-1 draw with Bulgaria; the first point by an African team at a World Cup.

The other debutants, who took the Asian place, were Israel, who had come close to qualifying in 1958 when a series of countries refused to play against them for political reasons. This time North Korea, one of the stars of 1966, refused to enter their group so Israel disposed of both New Zealand and Australia to progress. Having reached the finals they drew with Sweden and then unexpectedly held the Italians—the team that would end up as runners-up— to a goalless draw. After 1970 the Israelis were cast out of the Asian Football Conference and have been part of UEFA ever since, however they have not qualified again.

BACK HOME

Yet again England were the sole representatives from British shores, automatically qualifying as champions and their reign came to a sticky end in León against the obdurate Germans. However, the most memorable game for England not just in 1970 but also probably since, was their group clash with Brazil. This group was the first to be dubbed 'The Group of Death' as it also included Czechoslovakia who were runners-up in 1962 and Romania. This game had so many dimensions to it that it is difficult to pick out any singular one. It featured a truly masterful performance by Bobby Moore in which he kept many of the Brazilian's best players in check through a combination of astute positioning, keen anticipation and superbly timed tackles. And of course there was *that* Gordon Banks save, which simply defies not only logic but also some of the fundamental laws of physics no matter how many times you watch it.

Anyway the Brazilians' narrow, well-earned victory and that iconic picture of Moore and Pelé embracing as they swapped shirts in mutual admiration has resonated for many decades. As Pelé said later: "That photo has gone around the world. I think it was very important for football. We demonstrate that it's a sport. Win or lose, the example, the friendship, you must pass these on to other players, to the next generation." That moment felt like the mantle was being passed between two great teams and so it proved as Brazil succeeded England as World Champions a few weeks later with their emphatic win against Italy in Mexico City.

FOOTNOTE

To add to the majesty of Mexico 1970 even the balls used carried a certain class that has rarely, if ever, been matched. It was the first time that Adidas had been involved in the manufacture of the official match balls and they could hardly have started more impressively. The Adidas Telstar, with its simple but beautiful black pentagons and white hexagons made for an indelible image. It was almost mesmeric in its flight as it flashed across our screens, adding to the exotic feel of the tournament.

The ball was designed to be more visible on black-and-white televisions, as this was the first World Cup when matches were broadcast live across the world. Mind you even in colour they look fantastic. There have been many more elaborate designs and much more colour since 1970 but none have made quite the impact of the Telstar. It was such a success that the design was replicated in 1974 with a couple of minor tweaks and it has been resurrected for Russia 2018, with the FIFA blurb making a nod to the original classic. "The Telstar 18 evokes unforgettable memories of the 1970 World Cup and of legends like Pelé, Gerd Müller, Giacinto Facchetti, Pedro Rocha and Bobby Moore."

1974

HOST
West Germany

CITIES
Berlin, Dortmund, Dusseldorf, Frankfurt,
Gelsenkirchen, Hamburg, Hannover,
Munich, Stuttgart

DEBUTANTS (4)
Australia, East Germany, Haiti, Zaire

FINAL
Sunday 7 July, Olympiastadion, Munich (75,200)

NETHERLANDS (1) 1
Neeskens
V
WEST GERMANY (2) 2
Breitner, Müller
(Half-time score in brackets)

TOTAL ATTENDANCE
1,865,724 over 38 matches (Average 49,098)

TOP GOALSCORER (7)
Grzegorz Lato, Poland

"I PLAYED 18 YEARS IN TOP FOOTBALL AND 17 TIMES FOR SWEDEN BUT THAT MOMENT AGAINST CRUYFF WAS THE PROUDEST MOMENT OF MY CAREER. I THOUGHT I'D WIN THE BALL FOR SURE, BUT HE TRICKED ME. I WAS NOT HUMILIATED. I HAD NO CHANCE. CRUYFF WAS A GENIUS."

Jan Olsson, the Swedish right back on his experience of THAT turn.

INTRODUCTION

After the golden memories of Mexico, the next tournament was always going to struggle by comparison. The weather was a contributory factor with the blazing sunshine and searing heat of 1970 replaced by brooding clouds that produced plenty of soggy pitches in the latter stages. The colour was provided by the assorted rainwear of the spectators who were often dressed in cagoules of various shades as the rain lashed down. The football itself was also a pale imitation with the much-changed Brazilian team not the free spirits they were four years earlier. They limped unconvincingly to a showdown with The Netherlands, who were the most attractive team of tournament, before being dispatched by them with a fair degree of ease.

The Dutch were the only team which came close to replacing Brazil's flair as they featured the incomparable Johan Cruyff who gave us his eponymous turn and much more besides. It would be wrong to think of the Dutch as Cruyff and some bit-part players. The likes of Ruud Krol, Rob Rensenbrink and Arie Haan were all excellent footballers who were encouraged by Rinus Michels to play with freedom and a certain degree of flexibility. Thus the concept of Total Football was introduced to a global audience and won many converts during both this and the 1978 tournament.

Aside from the lack of a supreme team and the inclement weather the real dampener was the change to the format, which smacked of petty-minded tinkering by you know who. Rather than the cut and thrust of knock-out matches after the first round, there were two groups of four which battled it out to reach the final. Not since 1950 had a similar system been used and the tournament suffered as a result. The call to return to quarter-finals and semi-finals fell on deaf ears as FIFA persisted with this format until 1978 and persisted with a second round of groups in 1982 albeit with semi-finals, much to the chagrin of most of the audience. But when has popularity and common sense ever been an issue?

DEBUTANTS

The next tranche of countries trying their luck for the first time included Australia and three teams for whom this would be their only World Cups to date. East Germany would of course cease to exist after unification in 1990 but they made the most of this fleeting appearance becoming the only side to beat their neighbours and eventual winners, West Germany. That first-round victory was quite a coup and their candle flickered briefly before being extinguished in the second round, how they must have wished for a quarter-final rather than having to compete in a group that consisted of three of the strongest teams – Argentina, Brazil and the Netherlands, which gave them little chance of progressing.

Haiti had come within a whisker of qualifying for the 1970 World Cup but lost out to El Salvador in a play-off after their incendiary win against Honduras. Their passage to Germany via the CONACAF qualifiers came courtesy of Mexico suffering a resounding 4-0 defeat to Trinidad & Tobago in their penultimate game. This meant that even defeat to Mexico in their final game could not stop the Haiti qualifying. At last the most famous Haitian to play in the World Cup would no longer be somebody who represented another country. Joe Gaetjans, who scored America's winner against England in 1950, was supplanted by a new hero in Emmanuel Sanon and just like in Belo Horizonte it was a goal against one of the larger, more established football countries that established his reputation.

Nobody gave the Haitians a hope in their first game against an Italian side who had been finalists in 1970 and built a fearsome reputation for a formidable defence—they had not conceded a goal for a dozen matches stretching over almost two years. Dino Zoff, the keeper, was protected by a proud defensive system that had not been beaten for 1,096 minutes (just over 18 hours). At the same time Zoff's club side Juventus had racked up just over 10 hours without conceding a goal, so in total he had been on the field of play for over 28 hours since he last had to pick the ball out of the net.

Unsurprisingly, Zoff extended his clean sheet by another 45 minutes in Munich and at half-time he was surely eyeing the next landmark of 20 unbeaten hours for Italy. But just a minute into the second period Sanon latched on to a through ball, brushed off the attentions of the floundering Luciano Spinosi before coolly rounding Zoff and slotting the ball into the net. The puff of chalk as the ball crossed the line seemed a fitting tribute. Cue unconfined joy especially from the Haitian bench who were all leaping in the air with undisguised incredulity. That the Italians recovered to win 3-1 was almost irrelevant, Sanon had broken the spell and he was voted Haitian Athlete of the Century on the back of it.

With its guaranteed slot now established, Africa's representatives were Zaire who did not cover themselves in glory. They lost all three games without scoring a goal and were thumped 9-0 by Yugoslavia prior to facing the World Champions. It was against Brazil that one of their players also provided a lasting image of this World Cup but not quite in the same vein as Sanon. When Mwepu Ilunga broke rank from the defensive wall in the face of a Brazilian free-kick it looked like a false start in a 100 metre race but Mwepu did not pull up as expected to return to the wall he continued until he reached the untouched ball and without further ado smashed it downfield.

He subsequently explained in an interview in 2010 that this was no rush of blood to the head. It was the result of a grievance about the non-payment of bonuses. "I did that deliberately. I did not have a reason to continue getting injured while those who

will benefit financially were sitting on the terraces watching."
Whether it achieved the desired effect is a moot point but his bizarre
intervention certainly established him in the World Cup lexicon.

In contrast, Australia's debut went under the radar with barely
anything of note and hardly a flicker of excitement in their two
defeats and a goalless draw with Chile. They are one of the dirty
dozen countries, ranging from Belgium and Bolivia in 1930 to the
most recent, Trinidad & Tobago in 2006, which failed to score
in their first World Cup.

HOME NATIONS

It was role reversal for England and Scotland as the former fell at the
last hurdle when they failed to beat Poland on an infamous night at
Wembley. Polish keeper Jan Tomaszewski, derided as 'The Clown'
by Brian Clough, continuously denied the English. The bitter irony
was that the Polish goal was gifted to them by a catastrophic error
by Peter Shilton who Clough would sign for Nottingham Forest
four years later. Poland went on to prove that they were a decent
side with players like Grzegorz Lato, who became the tournament's
top scorer, and the stylish Kazimierz Deyna looking comfortable
on the biggest stage. They ended up winning the third placed
play-off against Brazil and one cannot imagine England would
have got that far.

So for the first time England failed to qualify and it was left
to Scotland to keep the British end up. They performed creditably
earning draws against Yugoslavia and, more impressively, Brazil,
finishing on the same points as their two rivals. However, their
failure to put group whipping boys Zaire to the sword ultimately
cost them as they went out on inferior goal difference. Had they
beaten Zaire by one more goal they would have qualified at Brazil's
expense. Although they did not make the second round they did
become the first country to remain unbeaten but fail to make it past
the first round, which is an achievement of sorts.

So British participation in the latter stages of the tournament was
limited to a referee and that man was Jack Taylor who was chosen

for the final between West Germany and Netherlands. Again there was a hint of controversy as Taylor awarded a penalty to the Dutch after just one minute; the closest the Germans had got to touching the ball was Uli Hoeness' lunge at Cruyff as he was upended in the penalty area. Amazingly, in the tenth World Cup final this was the first penalty to be awarded and it is also the fastest goal scored in a final. Taylor's decision was right but it took some courage to do so in Munich on such a prestigious occasion. It was not even the first decision he had to make as just before kick-off he noticed that there were no corner flags so they had to be found. Suffice to say it was a busy start for Taylor.

Johan Neeskens dispatched the penalty and the Dutch enjoyed the ascendancy with their customary swagger and élan but crucially they did not score a second. Not content with giving the first penalty in a final, Taylor then awarded the second some 20 minutes later. The Dutch, and Cruyff in particular, felt the penalty to the hosts was a way of balancing things up. An accusation that Taylor refutes categorically: "What really does annoy me is the suggestion that I gave it to even things up. It was a trip or an attempted trip and the laws of the game are that's a penalty." After Paul Breitner had equalised from the spot Müller did what he usually did, snapping up a chance inside the box with a swivel and low shot that smacked of efficiency rather than beauty. Regardless of aesthetics Müller's goal put the Germans into the lead and one that they never looked like surrendering.

RED CARDS AND RED POLITICS

After the lack of sendings-offs in the 1970 World Cup the dubious honour of receiving the first red card at the World Cup finals fell on Chilean Carlos Caszely. In Germany's opening match, Caszely reacted badly to a pretty rough tackle and in the tradition of the Battle of Santiago his retaliation was not subtle as he executed a flying kick and, much to his embarrassment, he was given that fateful red card.

Caszely was no stranger to rebellion as he was an active opponent of General Pinochet who had seized control of Chile from the Marxist government of Salvador Allende the year before the World Cup. When the players were introduced to Pinochet, Caszely did not exactly aim a kick at the dictator but he did make a point of shunning him. "A cold shiver went down my back from seeing this Hitler-like figure with five guys behind him," Caszely later recalled. "When he started coming closer I put my hand behind me and didn't give it to him."

In fact Chile had qualified for the World Cup partly because of Pinochet's coup when the Soviet Union team refused to travel for the second leg of their play-off in protest at the new regime, which had broken off diplomatic relations with Moscow. FIFA insisted that the game should go ahead but only the Chilean team turned up—they kicked off, walked the ball into the net and then were awarded the tie. As with most World Cups there were always kinks in the qualification system, primarily caused by political manoeuvres of one sort or the other.

FOOTNOTE

Playing for that impressive Polish side was a centre back who must have the most apposite name for the position in which he played. Jerzy Gorgoń was never going to be a nippy winger or a cultured midfield player, he just had to be a massive centre back. At 6'4" he certainly fitted the bill and with 55 caps, gold and silver Olympic medals plus the third place in Germany he clearly wasn't just a pretty name. For those who weren't paying attention in Greek mythology classes the three Gorgons were terrible monsters with snakes in their hair.

Not only was Gorgoń blessed with the perfect name but he also had the perfect mane. His blond curly locks somehow making him look even more like a man mountain and there could have been the odd serpent lurking in there somewhere. There was the odd criticism of Gorgoń footballing talent and one man stands out in his disrespectful dismissal of the defender as 'a donkey'.

Of course, as we have seen, this was not Brian Clough's only *faux pas* when assessing the relative abilities of Polish players.

1978

HOST
Argentina

CITIES
Buenos Aires, Cordoba, Mar Del Plata, Mendoza, Rosario

DEBUTANTS (2)
Iran, Tunisia

FINAL
Sunday 25 June, Estadio Monumental, Buenos Aires (71,483)

ARGENTINA (1) 3
Kempes 2, Bertoni

V

NETHERLANDS (1) 1
Nanninga

(1-1 after 90 minutes, result after extra time)

TOTAL ATTENDANCE
1,545,764 over 38 games. (Average 40,678)

TOP GOALSCORER (6)
Mario Kempes, Argentina

"I HONESTLY THINK THAT IF SCOTLAND, PROVIDED THAT WE PLAY WITH REASONABLE FORM AT ALL, WE WILL QUALIFY AND I THINK A MEDAL OF SOME SORT WILL COME AND I PRAY AND HOPE THAT IT IS THE GOLD ONE."

Ally MacLeod on his team's prospects prior to leaving for Argentina.

INTRODUCTION

The sight of toilet rolls being thrown from the terraces of English football grounds in the 1970s is one of those curious quirks whose origin is never quite explained. They were routinely hurled on to the pitch mostly before and occasionally during games as a sign of spectator feistiness, maybe based on a desire to be more involved in the action. When Argentina opened their campaign against Hungary in Buenos Aires on 2 June 1978 the sight of cascading ticker tape engulfing the stands put all those toilet rolls into perspective. The Estadio Monumental was transformed into a shimmering cauldron and in the face of this spectacular display from the Argentinian fans, the end was nigh for the relatively pathetic sight of the odd toilet roll forlornly flapping around the goal post.

Talking of goal posts the other unusual sight for World Cup spectators was the black bands that encircled the base of every post. There have been countless theories as to why they were in place, the most convincing of which was researched by David Forrest for *In Bed With Maradona*. Forrest tracked down one of the groundsmen from 1978 who explained that that the bands were memorials for the thousands of 'the disappeared'— those people who had been taken away by the military junta and, never to be seen again, assumed murdered. Yet again politics had made its mark on the football landscape as the simmering resentment of the ordinary people was expressed in this unique demonstration.

The looming presence of the Argentinian military cast a shadow over the tournament and many believe that this led to decisive favouritism shown to the host nation. There were certainly a host of incidents that aroused suspicions. From the opening match when two Hungarians were sent off despite reports suggesting they were more sinned against than sinning, to the all too convenient Peruvian capitulation against Argentina in the last group game of the second round which meant the hosts progressed to the final on goal difference at Brazil's expense. The recent admission by one of those Peruvian players, José Velásquez that six of his teammates were indeed bribed to throw the game is the latest in a long line of such claims.

Then there was the fuss made by the Argentinians before the final over René Van de Kerkhof's forearm cast being a danger to the players. It seemed odd that this had somehow escaped the attention of any officials in the previous matches when Van de Kerkhof had played with the same cast. The delay to the kick-off unsettled the Dutch and fired up the already passionate home crowd with Argentina eventually prevailing in extra time thanks to Mario Kempes' double. Kempes took his tally to six with those two goals securing the Golden Boot in the process and so becoming the first player on a winning team to top the individual goal scoring charts outright. Only two other players have achieved this and the next one would come in the following World Cup in Spain.

DEBUTANTS

The African and Asian qualifiers both made significant progress for their respective confederations. Few could have predicted how well the Tunisians would perform after they were drawn in a group with West Germany and Poland, the winners and the third-placed team from 1974 respectively, as well as Mexico. They became the first African nation to win a game at a World Cup and it was no streaky, slender victory as they comprehensively outplayed Mexico to win 3-1. They followed that landmark with a narrow loss to Poland courtesy of a single Lato goal before earning a draw with

West Germany. Finally, African countries would be treated with respect rather than the mixture of condescension and contempt that had greeted them before. The year before Pelé himself declared that there would be an African World Cup winner. Although the Brazilian may have been a bit hasty and we are still waiting for that prediction to come true, it is not as outlandish as it sounds.

Iran was another country in the middle of political turmoil as they were in the midst of the Islamic Revolution led by Ayatollah Khomeini, which ousted the Shah. The players could have been forgiven for having other things on their mind and their opening 3-0 defeat to the Dutch was understandable, after all this was the team that had finished runners-up in 1974 and would do so again in Argentina. The Iranian's next game was against the Scots who were licking their wounds from a 3-1 opening-game defeat to Peru. Here was the perfect opportunity for Scotland to get back on track with a convincing win.

However, the Iranians had other ideas. Despite conceding the opening goal courtesy of a tragicomic cock-up between Nasser Hejazi the goalkeeper and defender Andranik Eskandarian which led to the latter putting through his own net, Iran did not crumble and Scotland were not able to take advantage of their opponent's misfortune. The equaliser came on the hour when Iraj Danaeifard rifled in a shot from a tight angle between the near post and keeper Alan Rough. It was no great surprise as Iran had been applying pressure and they held out for a fully merited and historic draw. That they then succumbed rather meekly to Peru, losing their final Group match 4-1, could not detract from their first World Cup adventure. As for Scotland, they had plumbed new depths.

HOME NATIONS

For the second successive time England flunked their qualification. Alf Ramsey had left in the wake of the previous unsuccessful campaign, to be replaced by Don Revie. However, he abandoned ship midway through qualification, leaving for an easier and much more financially rewarding life in that hotbed of international football, the United Arab Emirates. Revie's desertion made him Public Enemy Number One for a while.

So it was again left to Scotland. A few months after Revie's inelegant departure Scotland also changed managers as Ally MacLeod took over from Willie Ormond with a couple of qualifying games remaining. Qualification was secured by a controversial victory at Anfield against a Welsh team convinced they had been victims of a harsh penalty award and the Scots left for Argentina with a decent side and on a wave of national optimism and their manager predicting they would win a medal. Their bubble burst against Peru, with the 29 year-old Teófilo Cubillas their chief tormentor. A player considered to be past his best was facing a Scottish midfield featuring a couple of thirtysomethings in Don Masson and Bruce Rioch. One of MacLeod's failings was his loyalty to certain players and the Scottish fans certainly did not suffer from any misplaced loyalty as they turned on their manager with some venom following this weak display.

The recriminations had only just started when further ignominy was heaped on the Scots. After the Peruvian match Archie Gemmill was chosen to undertake a drugs test but he was so dehydrated he could not produce a urine sample so Willie Johnston was chosen instead. Johnston tested positive for a banned stimulant and although he claimed it was part of a hay fever remedy he was sent home in disgrace adding to the beleaguered MacLeod's problems. As Johnston waspishly pointed out on his return, given the abject nature of the team's performance against Peru it could hardly been a performance-enhancing drug.

Worse was to follow when the Iranian debacle completely derailed Scotland's chances of making the second round. Somehow they recovered to produce one of their best performances in a World Cup beating the Dutch despite going behind to a Rob Rensenbrink penalty – the 1,000th in the World Cup. Of course this extraordinary win featured that most Dutch-like goal from Gemmill as he jinked and danced his way through a series of half-hearted challenges before the coolest of chips over the keeper. As the Cruyff Turn became the totem of Total Football then

Gemmill's effort was a symbol of Futile Football. It was a victory as unexpected as it was glorious but it was not quite enough for the Scots to reach the second round. The 3-2 win put a thin gloss on a wretched campaign and there was to be no medal of any colour nor a triumphant homecoming for Ally's Tartan Army to match their overblown departure of a few weeks before when they had indulged themselves in a vainglorious lap of honour around Hampden Park. As an example of hubris it was hard to beat and in stark contrast to their limp arrival back in Scotland.

The Welsh had, like the English, failed to qualify in 1978 but it was their refereeing representative who arguably made the most significant Home-nation contribution to the tournament with a decision that has been viewed a million times and challenged a million times more. Clive Thomas was in charge of Brazil's opening group match with Sweden, which like so many such games was meandering towards a tame draw when a late Brazil corner was floated into the penalty area to be met by a thumping Zico header that looked to have been the last act of the game.

Thomas had other ideas, having blown the full time whistle as the ball was in the air and just before it reached Zico. The Brazilians were aghast at the decision and despite the pandemonium which ensued the man in the middle was in no mood to back down. Ironically, José Reinaldo de Lima's equaliser for Brazil was scored in added time in the first half, with the commentator noting that Thomas let that one count despite already checking his watch in the build-up. The other thorny issue was that Zico's 'goal' was timed at 45:08 so Thomas had not made any allowance for even a single minute of added time, which would be difficult to imagine being possible.

Thomas has always maintained that his decision was correct and it might well have been in the strict interpretation of the laws but surely it would have been more practical either to end the game before the corner was taken or allow it to play out. In an interview with the *You Are the Ref* website Thomas himself acknowledged that this would not happen today. "Now, no matter how many matches you watch on the television you will never see the referee blow his whistle for full-time while the ball is in the area. So do I understand why people disagree with me? Yes, but I also know the very same people also say 'we respect you because you're honest'. And you can't better that, can you?"

FOOTNOTE

That 1,000th goal by Rensenbrik was scored in the 11th tournament, coming in the 293rd game, which equates to a healthy average of 3.4 goals per game at that point. It took just seven tournaments to record the next 1,000 with Marcus Allbäck's first equaliser for Sweden against England in Cologne in 2006 the 2,000th World Cup goal. But of course there had been a significant increase in the number of games played to achieve that landmark. It took almost 400 games to score those second 1,000 goals as they arrived at a much lower rate of 2.5 goals per game. However, it took fewer tournaments because the number of games per tournament increased as the number of participating countries has steadily increased from just 13 in Uruguay in 1930. In 1998 the number of countries competing was expanded from 24 to 32, so now there are 64 games at each World Cup, and FIFA has announced that from 2026 the World Cup, will expand again to an unwieldy 48 teams.

1982

HOST
Spain

CITIES
Alicante, Barcelona, Bilbao, A Coruña, Elche, Gijon, Madrid, Malaga, Oviedo, Seville, Valencia, Valladolid, Vigo, Zaragoza

DEBUTANTS (5)
Algeria, Cameroon, Honduras, Kuwait, New Zealand

FINAL
Sunday 11 July, Bernabeu, Madrid (90,000)

ITALY (0) 3
Rossi, Tardelli, Altobelli

V

WEST GERMANY (0) 1
Breitner

(Half-time score in brackets)

TOTAL ATTENDANCE
2,109,692 over 52 games. (Average 40,571)

TOP GOALSCORER (6)
Paolo Rossi, Italy

"I OBSERVED HIS BEHAVIOUR, THE WAY HE CLASHED WITH DOMINIQUE ROCHETEAU AND DIDIER SIX. I THOUGHT HE WAS VERY HYPED UP, VERY EXCITABLE. I REMARKED ON THIS TO THE OTHER PLAYERS ON THE BENCH."

Patrick Battiston's observations on Harald Schumacher
before their infamous clash in the semi-final.

INTRODUCTION

This was thankfully the last World Cup that persisted with the cumbersome and flawed system of a second round of group games and featured one of the great semi-finals, which helpfully emphasised how straight knockout football could be the platform for the most captivating drama. By contrast the majority of the second round games were rather underwhelming, England's pair of goalless draws did not exactly get the pulses racing. Just to balance things out there was a quite wonderful match in the most exciting second round group of all those contested over the four tournaments to use the format, but this was very much the exception that proved the rule.

Group C had all the ingredients required for thrilling football. All three teams were World Cup winners including Brazil and Argentina, the two South American giants, and Italy, one of Europe's finest teams. All three games were high in quality and entertainment with a healthy dose of great goals. When Italy met Brazil in Barcelona everything was up for grabs, both sides having beaten Argentina, who had a player sent off in each of those matches. It was almost like a quarter-final, although it wasn't quite a winner-takes-all-showdown as a draw was enough for Brazil to progress.

All the elements of a classic encounter were encapsulated in this thrilling match: the fluctuation in fortunes, great goals and a stunning individual performance allied with a dash of redemption. Brazil twice pegged back Italy and although the second from Falcão was probably the more spectacular as he smashed the ball in from the edge of the area, the first from Sócrates was the result of a superb interchange between the great doctor and Zico.

Paolo Rossi, who had only just returned from a two-year ban for his part in the Totonero match-fixing scandal, was understandably rusty in the early matches having played just three games for Juventus at the tail-end of the domestic season. From these unpromising circumstances he managed to score as accomplished a hat-trick as any in World Cup history—a precise far post header, a neat finish after taking advantage of a slip in the Brazilian defence and a swivelling shot on the edge of the six-yard box. It was not exactly the perfect hat-trick but it was mighty close. Rossi followed that up with a brace in the semi and the opener in the final. He was the tournament's top scorer becoming only the second player on the winning side to be awarded the Golden Boot after Kempes in 1978, and 34 years later he was inducted into the Italian Football Hall of Fame.

The Italians' splendid victory over the Germans in the final drew universal acclaim after the Patrick Battiston/Harald Schumacher incident that had marred the semi-final. Schumacher did not just flatten the Frenchman when he charged recklessly out of his goal, he poleaxed him without any regard for either the ball or the man. Battiston was knocked unconscious, suffered horrific injuries including losing a couple of teeth, a cracked vertebra and breaking a few ribs. Schumacher escaped any punishment, not even a yellow card, and this lack of action remains one of the most extreme derelictions of duty by a referee throughout the history of football let alone the World Cup.

The fact that the semi-final was the very first World Cup game to be decided by penalties was pretty much lost amid the uproar surrounding that Schumacher challenge and the horrifying injuries that the Frenchman suffered. If ever there was a victory for the football gods then Italy's triumph in Madrid was it. Retribution was served by the Italians' comprehensive 3-1 win and Marco

Tardelli's memorable wide-eyed, joyous celebration was the perfect antidote to one of the more disgraceful episodes. The excellence of Tardelli's left foot strike that gave the Italians a 2-0 lead was immediately overshadowed by his unadulterated delight as he ran with knees and arms pumping before being engulfed by his team mates on the sideline.

DEBUTANTS

Debuting countries generally find a way of making an impression during their first tournament, although not always for the most positive reasons. Kuwait certainly did not do so through flowing football or having any outstanding players. Having achieved respectability with their opening draw against Czechoslovakia their next game against France offered a different sort of challenge. The French, who boasted one of the most impressive midfield quartets of the modern era in Jean Tigana, Alain Giresse, Bernard Genghini and the incomparable Michel Platini, often purred through the gears with rarely matched elegance.

Kuwait were no match for their opponents and were 3-0 down just after half-time and so the remaining 40 minutes were very much a damage limitation exercise. From that point of view, all was going pretty well and they had even sneaked in a consolation goal before Giresse finished off a move to restore the three-goal lead. It was pretty inconsequential but that did not prevent the Kuwaitis from claiming that they had stopped playing because of a whistle, the only problem was that whatever they heard was nothing to do with the referee, who awarded the goal.

The President of the Kuwaiti FA, who just happened to be the emir, started to agitate in the stands beckoning the team to come off. As if that was not enough he then came down to the pitch along with a delegation to argue the toss. By then the Spanish constabulary were feeling left out so came on to add their tuppence. The commotion eventually died down and the referee retrospectively disallowed the goal, which only served to rile the French manager Michel Hidalgo who was apoplectic at the intervention and threw his own hissy fit. After the resumption of play the French almost inevitably got their fourth anyway in the final minute.

Like Kuwait, Algeria were handed a tough assignment in their group against Austria, Chile and first of all West Germany. There was to be no encroachment from external forces this time with the mayhem instead being wrought by the players on the pitch as they not only upset the applecart but smashed it to smithereens. Having taken the most surprising of leads through Rabah Madjer in the 53rd minute order was soon restored by Karl-Heinz Rummenigge's equaliser. But Algeria retook the lead within a couple of minutes when Lakhdar Belloumi scored. Few would have thought the Algerians could hold out for another 20 minutes but that is exactly what they did and one of the most seismic World Cup shocks was complete.

Although they lost to Austria in their next match, their 3-2 win against Chile in their last game put them on the verge of an amazing qualification. But there was to be another shock in this group and this was to be a much more unwholesome affair. Germany and Austria, playing the day after Algeria's final game, knew that a 1-0 win for the Germans would see them both qualify, and that is what they conspired to produce, squeezing the Algerians out on goal difference. So much for principles, national pride and sporting decency, one can only wonder what Matthias Sindelar, the Austrian-born player who refused to play for Germany after the Nazi annexation of his country, would have made of such chicanery between the two countries.

The only good thing to come out of the Disgrace of Gijón, as this sordid saga became known, was that FIFA finally realised the folly of teams playing their final group matches at different times. From 1986 onwards the last two games in each group would kick off simultaneously to avoid the possibility of any repeat of such dubious shenanigans.

Cameroon became the first African country to remain undefeated at a World Cup but unfortunately for Roger Milla and co this was not enough to see them qualify. Their three draws with Peru,

Poland and eventual winners Italy left them third in the group and on the same points as the Italians but they went out not on inferior goal difference but because they had scored one goal less than Italy. This tightest of margins has only been the decisive factor on two other occasions and by coincidence one of those was in the same year when Spain qualified ahead of Yugoslavia. It was incredibly tough on the Indomitable Lions but they did not have to wait too long to make their mark at a World Cup.

The other two debutants, Honduras and New Zealand, did not quite make the same impression as both were winless and finished bottom of their groups. Despite this Honduras must have relished the humiliating thrashing that their bitter rivals El Salvador endured against Hungary. The Hungarians' 10-1 victory was the only time a team has got into double figures at a World Cup. The game also featured the quickest hat-trick the wonderfully-named Hungarian substitute László Kiss scoring three in seven minutes. Honduras themselves collected a couple of points from draws with Northern Ireland and Spain and a narrow loss to Yugoslavia while New Zealand suffered three heavy defeats conceding a dozen goals.

HOME NATIONS

With England returning after their two successive qualification failures, there was some nervousness about how Ron Greenwood's men would fare, which was not eased by having France as their first opponents. It took less than a minute to dispel such uncertainty as Bryan Robson scored the fastest World Cup goal when he hooked in a cross at the far post after just 27 seconds. That 3-1 win was a platform for a straightforward qualification to the second round as England also beat Czechoslovakia and Kuwait; the only time they have recorded a 100% record in first round. Having started with a bang they ended on a whimper as two goalless draws against West Germany and Spain in the second group stage led to the end of their involvement, unbeaten but ultimately undistinguished.

After 1974 Scotland knew all about going home without suffering defeat and they were becoming accustomed to this World Cup lark as Spain was their third tournament in a row. Having given New Zealand a solid shellacking in the first game they even had the audacity to take the lead against Brazil through the unlikely David Narey who scored a goal that would not have looked out of place in the Maracanã. If you are only going to score one goal for your country you might as well make it a stunner. But that impertinence was soon put in its place as Brazil clicked into gear with four goals including a simply sumptuous free kick by Zico that left Alan Rough flatfooted, flabbergasted and flummoxed. Failure to beat Russia in the final game meant another early exit for the Scots.

Both England and Scotland were disappointed and disappointing, but that could not be said of the other Home Nation involved. Northern Ireland were back after a gap of 24 years and they certainly made up for lost time. The zenith came when they upset the odds and the hosts on a steamy night in Valencia. Gerry Armstrong grabbed the winner, slamming the ball home after keeper Luis Arconada palmed Billy Hamilton's cross into his path. Somehow they survived the Spanish onslaught even after Mal Donaghy was sent off with 30 minutes to play.

It was not quite on the same scale as the Algerians' humbling of the Germans but it was still a major upset. Unbelievably the Northern Irish topped the group and maintained their 100% record of qualifying for the second phase. In the second round their 2-2 draw with Austria gave them a sniff of a chance of reaching the semi-finals but a fast-improving France proved to be a step too far. During their campaign Norman Whiteside became the youngest ever player to make a World Cup Finals appearance at the tender age of 17 years and 41 days. To put that into context Whiteside was born in 1965, seven years after Northern Ireland's first foray, and a year after the team's goalkeeper Pat Jennings had made his international debut. Talking of keepers of a certain age, in the final Dino Zoff became the oldest player to win the World Cup at the not-so-tender age of 40 years and 113 days.

FOOTNOTE

The World Cup draw has become quite an elaborate operation in recent years with a whole host of celebrities and ex-players congregating in front of a worldwide TV audience to determine who plays whom. Nothing will ever quite plumb the depths of the farce that took place in Madrid in December 1981. Even FIFA, not an organisation known for self-criticism, conceded in their official record that all did not go according to plan: "The draw ceremony in Madrid is unfortunately best remembered (or forgotten) for a mishap with one of the revolving drums containing the mini-footballs with the teams' names and the confusion that ensued in an effort to keep the South American qualifiers apart in the first round."

It was not just those drums that had a sticky moment as the malfunctioning equipment embarrassed not only the schoolchildren who had the responsibility of ferrying the balls but also the FIFA officials, who included the newly appointed general secretary who was presiding over his first draw. Sepp Blatter's wriggling humiliation was a sight to behold as the need for a re-draw rendered the whole fiasco appear more like a village fête, and not a very well run fête at that.

1986

HOST
Mexico

CITIES
Calisco, Guadalajara, Irapuato, Leon, Mexico City, Monterrey, Nezhualcoyotl, Puebla, Queretaro, Toluca, Zapopan

DEBUTANTS (3)
Canada, Denmark, Iraq

FINAL
Sunday 29 June, Azteca, Mexico City (114,850)

ARGENTINA (1) 3
Brown, Valdano, Burruchaga

V

WEST GERMANY (0) 2
Rummenigge, Voller
(Half-time score in brackets)

TOTAL ATTENDANCE
2,394,028 over 52 matches (Average 46,039)

TOP GOALSCORER (6)
Gary Lineker, England

"[THE GOAL WAS SCORED] A LITTLE WITH THE HEAD OF MARADONA AND A LITTLE WITH THE HAND OF GOD. ALTHOUGH WE HAD SAID BEFORE THE GAME THAT FOOTBALL HAD NOTHING TO DO WITH THE MALVINAS WAR, WE KNOW THAT THEY HAD KILLED A LOT OF ARGENTINE BOYS THERE, KILLED THEM LIKE LITTLE BIRDS. AND THIS WAS REVENGE."

Maradona on THAT goal.

INTRODUCTION

Mexico became the first country to host the World Cup twice after Colombia, the original hosts, pulled out for financial reasons. Although the 1986 tournament could never seriously be expected to match the peerless 1970 version, it had its moments and was rarely short of controversy or entertainment. Brazil briefly flickered into the sort of form with which they had graced the same stage 16 years earlier, with two of their most spectacular goals scored by their full back Josimar. In the group stage he beat Pat Jennings with an absolute beauty which the Northern Irish keeper could only watch in admiration and in the round of 16 he danced his way through the Polish defence before unleashing a venomous strike. Josimar's joyous celebrations mirrored those of Jairzinho in 1970 as he ran away with his arms raised to the skies in exultation.

However, Brazil were beaten in the quarter-finals by the French, losing out in a penalty shoot-out. As this was the welcome return to knock-out football it was faintly ironic that two of the other quarter-finals were also decided by penalties with fellow Europeans Belgium and West Germany also prevailing against Spain and Mexico respectively. Penalty shoot-outs are not to everyone's taste as they are the cruellest way to depart but the drama is inescapable and are preferable to any of the complicity that had besmirched the group system.

No player was more exciting nor as controversial as Diego Maradona who combined the most incredible skill with brazen, outrageous skullduggery. He was responsible for two of the greatest goals ever scored and one of the most treacherous acts all within the space of a few days, illustrating perfectly his uncanny capacity to be hero and villain and sometimes both in the same game. William Shakespeare would have had a field day with such a flawed genius, although the Argentinian was definitely more sinning than sinned against. He was instrumental in helping his team reach the final where they beat West Germany with a late goal. The Germans had mounted a comeback from 2-0 down but it wasn't enough and they joined the Dutch as being one of only two countries to lose consecutive finals. As an Englishman, seeing Maradona holding the trophy aloft was both fitting and gutting in equal measure. It was difficult to know what to do – applaud or scream.

DEBUTANTS

Denmark can lay claim to making one of the most impressive World Cup debuts winning their three group games before they were mauled by the Spaniards, and in particular Emilio 'The Vulture' Butragueño, in the Round of 16. Part of the reason why the Danes attracted immediate attention was the aesthetic appeal of their Hummel kit, which was as eye-catching as it was original. The red and white halves with their pin striped effect accentuated the silky football of the likes of Michael Laudrup, Prebjen Elkjær and Frank Arnesen. It is rare for a team making their first appearance to be so assured and measured but considering how the Danes would later gatecrash the Euros in 1992, they were clearly adept at arriving well prepared.

They beat Scotland 1-0 in their opening game before demolishing Uruguay 6-1 in a match that was beauty personified. It was just rewards for their free-flowing football and just desserts for the

South Americans' brutality. Miguel Bossio's assault on Laudrup that led to his dismissal midway through the first half was nearly as stupid as it was malicious, as he had only just been booked. The Dane got his revenge in the second half with a sublime goal as he ghosted through what was left of a ragged Uruguayan defence. When Denmark followed that up with a 2-0 win over West Germany they had quickly become everyone's second team. They took the lead against Spain in their next match but Butragueño had other ideas, scoring four times as Spain romped to a 5-1 win.

Neither Canada nor Iraq have much football pedigree and they did not exactly light up the tournament. Neither really threatened to claim a win but both were dogged, so avoided any serious damage and they ran some pretty good teams close. For example Canada held on for 79 minutes before conceding to France while the Iraqis managed to notch a goal in their 2-1 defeat to the Belgians. Neither country have managed to qualify since and it may be a while before either make their return to the World Cup arena.

HOME NATIONS

Just as in Spain, England, Scotland and Northern Ireland all qualified and it was a familiar tale with none of the trio really fulfilling their potential. It was Northern Ireland's turn to be paired with Brazil in the group and by chance they also had Spain and an opportunity to inflict further damage on the team they famously beat four years earlier. However, Brazil were too strong for them and ran out 3-0 winners while Spain exacted revenge with a 2-1 victory. The consolation of a solitary point from their 1-1 draw with Algeria was a disappointment for the Northern Irish after the exultation of their previous appearance.

As this was their fourth straight World Cup appearance Scotland must have started to become accustomed to how things panned out but this was actually one of their poorer collective performances. The death of Jock Stein during the qualifying game against Wales had been a massive shock to the system but his replacement Alex Ferguson had proved himself at club level with an unfashionable club. The Scot had transformed Aberdeen's fortunes as they challenged and overcame the Old Firm and even proved themselves in Europe by winning the Cup Winners Cup, beating no less a club than Real Madrid in the Final.

Even though Scotland had not qualified for the second round in each of the previous three World Cups, at least there had been the odd win to savour. There was no such luck this time round. After two narrow defeats to Denmark and West Germany they faced the uncompromising Uruguayans in their final group game. The South Americans outdid themselves when, less than a minute into the game José Batista let Gordon Strachan 'know he was there' with a scything challenge which left the diminutive Scottish midfielder in a crumpled heap. For his efforts Batista earned the fastest ever World Cup sending off and it is difficult to imagine anybody wresting that particular record off him. Despite the opposition being down to ten men for 89 minutes Scotland could not make the breakthrough and they departed the scene early yet again. Even Ferguson could not work his magic and he resigned soon afterwards.

England started their campaign miserably, losing anaemically to Portugal before stuttering to a goalless draw against the expected minnows of the group, Morocco. In fact Morocco topped the group and in so doing became the first African country to ever progress from the first round of a World Cup. They lost out by a single goal to West Germany in the last 16 but still left with heads held high. The same could not be said of Ray Wilkins who became the first English player to be sent off at a World Cup after he petulantly threw the ball towards the referee and having been booked only a few minutes earlier he was given a red card. It was hardly on the Uruguayan scale of foul play, but it was pretty inexcusable from one of the senior players in the squad who was not known for disciplinary problems.

The dismantling of Poland in the last group game courtesy of Gary Lineker's first-half hat-trick provided salvation and Lineker continued to lead England from the front with a brace against Paraguay and a goal against Argentina. His six goals were enough to win him the Golden Boot, a unique achievement for an Englishman. We all know how the showdown with Argentina finished as Maradona's "Hand of God" delivered the first blow to Bobby Robson's team just after half-time. Five minutes later he let his feet do the talking with that mazy run that bamboozled, befuddled and bemused a clutch of England players. England cursed their luck, Maradona and the referee Ben Nasser in equal measure but there was no hiding the fact that Argentina were the more accomplished side as they would prove by becoming the champions for the second time in three tournaments.

FOOTNOTE

As well as the deeds and misdeeds for which Maradona is remembered at the tournament is the photo of him being hacked down by South Korea's Huh Jung-moo. The image, which shows Maradona flying through the air, face wracked in pain, was captured in the teams' opening match which Argentina won 3-1. Twenty-four years later the two would lock horns again in 2010 World Cup in South Africa when Argentina again won comfortably, 4-1. This time Maradona and Huh were adversaries off the pitch rather than on it, as their country's head coaches, so there were not so many photo opportunities.

1990

HOST
Italy

CITIES
Bari, Bologna, Cagliari, Florence, Genoa, Milan, Naples, Palermo, Rome, Trieste, Udine, Verona

DEBUTANTS (3)
Costa Rica, Republic Of Ireland, United Arab Emirates

FINAL
Sunday 8 July, Stadio Olimpico, Rome (73,603)

ARGENTINA (0) 0
V
WEST GERMANY (0) 1
Brehme
(Half-time score in brackets)

TOTAL ATTENDANCE
2,516,176 over 52 matches (Average 48,388)

TOP GOALSCORER (6)
Salvatore Schillaci, Italy

"I THINK 1990 WAS HUGELY IMPORTANT TO FOOTBALL IN THIS COUNTRY. AFTER THAT EVERYONE BECAME INTERESTED IN FOOTBALL. IT WASN'T JUST WORKING-CLASS MEN IT WAS ALL CLASSES, WOMEN, KIDS—IT RETURNED TO THE FAMILY GAME IT SHOULD BE. BOBBY WAS AT THE HELM THEN AND THAT HELPED TO CEMENT HIS POPULARITY."

Gary Lineker

INTRODUCTION

The 1990 World Cup was a watershed moment for several reasons. English fans' memories are suitably tear-stained. Inspired and thrilled by the genius of Paul Gascoigne, then crushed by the yellow card that would have ruled him out of the final and tormented by the agony of Stuart Pearce and Chris Waddle's penalty misses. All washed down with a splash of Luciano Pavarotti. For once England had actually made a good impression, admittedly after a tentative start and were in with a chance of success but that proved elusive and being that close to glory seems a million miles away from where we are now. At least England did not come home empty-handed as they picked up the Fair Play award.

The final itself was one of the worst in the entire history of the World Cup, with neither side providing anything particularly positive or attractive during the tortuous, nay tedious, 90 minutes. Pedró Monzon became the first player to receive a red card in a final and to make doubly sure that we noticed Argentina had a second player, Gustavo Dezotti, sent off for good measure, or maybe that should be bad measure in this case.

It was entirely apposite that the only goal of the game was a penalty, as there was not enough invention or intention in open play to merit a goal of any other sort. So thanks to Andreas Brehme's 85th minute spot kick, the Germans avenged their defeat of four years previously in the only final contested by the same sides who met in the final of the previous tournament. That Franz Beckenbauer became the first man to captain and coach World Cup winners felt almost incidental and although it was the 14th staging, Argentina became the first finalist who failed to score. Since then five of the six finals have featured at least one team drawing a blank and in the 1994 World Cup final neither team troubled the scorers—the only time the final has ended in a goalless draw. This could be seen as the start of a more practical, dour age where winning was considered more important than style. From the land of Macchiavelli came a more Macchiavellian approach.

The whole tournament was a sterile affair as negative tactics seemed to have become the tactical *lingua franca* and there was very little in the way of attractive or stylish football on show. With an average of 2.2 goals per game this was the lowest-scoring World Cup. Oh for the heady days of 1954 when the average was more than double that. As a consequence FIFA introduced the law prohibiting goalkeepers from handling the ball after it was played back to them by a teammate thus closing off that particularly boring tactical means of stifling games.

Beneath this pall of negativity there were, of course, some uplifting moments and Cameroon provided a fair few. By becoming the first African nation to get to the quarter-finals they built on the progress made by the likes of Algeria and Morocco. In Roger Milla they had perhaps the greatest story of all. Milla was rescued from semi-retirement at the grand old age of 38 and became the definition of a super sub as he scored all four of his goals after coming off the from the bench against Romania and Colombia. His joyous, hip-gyrating celebrations around the corner flag were the perfect embellishment to this symbol of longevity.

Having become the oldest goal scorer at a World Cup, Milla then broke his own record at the 1994 tournament aged 42, although there was not so much of a celebratory feel as his goal came in a 6-1 hammering by Russia. His achievements were recognised when in 2007 he was voted the best African player of the last five decades. Not bad for a player who would not even have played in a World Cup were it not for the Cameroonian President's insistence and the coach bowing to political pressure.

RED MIST & RED CARDS

Alongside the oldest swinger in town the Cameroonians were not afraid to dish out some punishment as they proved in the opening game of the tournament against Argentina. They battered the World Champions into submission and gained a famous victory despite having two of their players sent off. The second red card was the result of a tackle by Benjamin Massing, on Claudio Caniggia was little short of GBH. As the Argentinian surged forward in the last few minutes of the match Cameroon's players attempted to take him out not once, not twice but three times. Such was the force of Massing's bodycheck that he lost a boot as Caniggia was left sprawling on the turf. The outraged Argentinians surrounded the referee, who allowed Massing time to replace his boot before sending him off.

So both the very first and last games of this World Cup featured a pair of dismissals, which was a unique way to top and tail the dirtiest of all tournaments. It was not just the Argentinians and the Cameroonians who were hell bent on crossing the line of legitimacy. The overall tally of 16 red cards in the 52 matches was as many as had been awarded in the previous three tournaments put together. This was the school of hard knocks and although the instructions handed to officials to stamp out foul play were undoubtedly a contributory factor, there still had to be foul play in the first place and there was plenty on display in Italy.

There was one other game that featured two red cards and this is the one that will go down in the annals of the filthiest, most disgusting behaviour of any World Cup. Any meeting between the Dutch and the Germans is laden with simmering rivalry but this last 16 match was laden with something even more unpleasant; Frank Rijkaard's spit.

The Dutchman and Rudi Völler had been engaged in a feud that had been rumbling on since the start of the game. Breaking point arrived when Rijkaard was booked for an uncharacteristically crude and agricultural foul on Völler, as this was his second yellow card of the tournament it meant that he would miss the quarter-final if the Dutch progressed. Clearly riled, Rijkaard then did something, which was equally out of character for such an elegant, composed and laid-back player. As he jogged back into position he spat into Völler's hair. This rightly enraged the German who was then booked for remonstrating with his assailant while he tried to show the evidence of Rijkaard's expectoration to the referee.

After the resulting free-kick was swung into the Dutch box Völler challenged the opposition keeper Hans Van Breukelen. Although it appeared to be a genuine attempt to get to the ball Rijkaard took exception to it and hauled the prostrate Völler off the ground while 'inadvertently' stamping on his foot. This angered Völler took exception to this and there was a fair bit of pushing between the two, which led to both men getting their marching orders.

There was still more to come as both were heading towards the dressing rooms, Rijkaard again decided to decorate Völler's perm with a further volley of spittle. Somehow Völler kept his cool and trotted past Rijkaard without trying to exact any revenge. In fact the two, who had been playing club football in Italy at the time for Roma and AC Milan respectively, were reconciled shortly afterwards as Rijkaard explained. "I always had respect for Rudi, but I went berserk when I saw that red card. I talked to him after the match and I apologised. I'm very happy that he accepted. I have no bad feelings about him now. We even posed for a very funny advert together years after." That advertisement for Dutch butter bizarrely completed one of the more unlikely reconciliations after one of the most unsavoury incidents.

DEBUTANTS

As they were one of the smallest countries by population to have
qualified for the World Cup, many people will have thought that
Costa Rica were there to make up the numbers, but it wasn't to
be. Their qualification from the CONACAF group was made a
whole lot easier when perennial qualifiers Mexico were disqualified
for fielding ineligible players. Facing Scotland in their first ever
game did not prove to overawe the Costa Ricans and under the
canny management of the experienced Yugoslav Bora Milutinović
they pulled off a shock. When they took the lead shortly after
half time it was assumed that the Scots would finally shake off
their torpor and assert their supremacy. However, it wasn't to
be and the Costa Ricans repelled the Scottish without undue
problems and just like Denmark in 1986 became one of the few
post-war debutants to win their opening game.

Just to prove that was not a freak result Costa Rica then gave
Brazil a run for their money with the only goal of the game a
scruffy finish by Müller and followed that up with a 2-1 win
in their last group game against Sweden thus ensuring their
place in the last 16. The aerial power of Czechoslovakia and in
particular Tomáš Skuhravý, who helped himself to a hat-trick,
put paid to the Costa Ricans' hopes of further progress. However,
their win against Scotland was not the last time that they would
embarrass a supposedly superior British team.

Having recruited World Cup winner Jack Charlton as their
manager, almost inevitably the Republic of Ireland's first opponent
was England. In a similar way to the Costa Ricans the Irish did
not suffer from any sense of inferiority. They were not unduly
disconcerted by Lineker's early strike and fully deserved Kevin
Sheedy's equaliser. Subsequent draws with the Dutch and the
Egyptians secured a last 16 place and their fourth draw led to
a penalty shoot-out victory over Romania and a quarter-final
against the home nation. In losing to a single Salvatore Schillaci
goal the Irish showed great courage and an innate ability to
scrap it out. Ultimately they lacked any real firepower but they

certainly served notice that they would always be difficult to beat.

The last of the debutants were the United Arab Emirates who were unlucky to be in a strong group with seasoned World Cup practitioners Colombia, Yugoslavia and West Germany. What they lacked in terms of experience on the pitch they more than made up for in the calibre of their managers, with two Brazilians taking the reins in quick succession. Carlos Alberto Parreira, took over from Mario Zagallo, a few months before the World Cup started. Zagallo had become the first person to win as both player, in 1958 and 1962, and as manager, in 1970 while Parriera would go on to lead Brazil to victory in 1994. However, the Brazilian magic did not quite rub off on the pitch as the UAE were beaten comfortably in all three of their games.

HOME NATIONS

England's pedestrian start in their group games with two draws and a narrow win over Egypt did not provide too much hope that this was going to be any improvement on their 1986 performance. The ridiculously late win against Belgium via David Platt's hooked volley was celebrated with more relief than euphoria. The thwarting of Cameroon owed as much to a very generous referee awarding the English two penalties as it did to Gary Lineker converting them. Then it was another showdown with West Germany, for their fourth meeting in their last five World Cup appearances. The devastating loss on penalties was not unexpected but it was nonetheless painful and it was all the more galling when their final with Argentina was such a damp squib.

As has already been mentioned, Scotland's start was even worse than England's and they did well to recover from their Costa Rican nightmare with a 2-1 win against Sweden, leaving all to play for in their final group game. Alas that was against Brazil and although a 1-0 loss was no disgrace it could not save them from yet another first-round exit when Costa Rica got the result they needed to send them into the last 16 instead.

FOOTNOTE

Some of the most enduring images of any major football tournament are the goal celebrations. By adding their own interpretation to the key art of goal scoring players can ensure they capture the public's imagination and although Italia 90 was not blessed with the sheer volume of goals, there was a plethora of individual moments of spontaneous and not-so-spontaneous delight. As already mentioned, Roger Milla's sudden affinity with the corner flags was a highlight as was the rapidly-assembled mountain of English players topped off by an incredulous Lineker that followed Platt's winner against Belgium.

Alongside these it was the unrestrained joy of the leading goal scorer Salvatore 'Toto' Schillaci that became the defining motif of this World Cup—something that we got to see half a dozen times. After scoring, Schillaci would summon up his innermost Tardelli spirit, wheeling away in unadulterated delight while adding a nice line in eye-popping mania to the mix.

Although he had had a good first season for Juventus, Schillaci was a late inclusion in the Italian squad. Initially he was not considered good enough to oust the likes of Gianluca Vialli and so he started on the bench. But just like Milla, he came on to devastating effect in the Italians' first match, scoring the only goal of the game against Austria. He then scored against Czechoslovakia in the last group match before grabbing further goals in the three knock out games. However, the Italians lost to Argentina on penalties in the semi-final and even though Schillaci scored from the spot in the third-placed match, he was not asked to take one in that fateful shootout.

He almost carried the host nation all the way but just as Italy's hopes were dashed so Schillaci's international career, which had started so explosively fizzled out and he only made a couple more appearances for his country. But the legacy lives on as the man himself describes: "The eyes, the eyes. Every time I meet people they always want me to do the 'wild eyes'. It was an instinctive gesture that has stuck in people's minds, and I have done it many,

many times." After his career petered away over the next few years he finally ended up going to the J-League as the first Italian to play club football in Japan, alongside the Golden Boot winner at the previous World Cup, Gary Lineker.

1994

HOST
USA

CITIES
Boston, Chicago, Dallas, Michigan, Orlando, Palo Alto, Pasadena, Rutherford (NJ), Washington

DEBUTANTS (3)
Greece, Nigeria, Saudi Arabia

FINAL
Sunday 17 July, Rose Bowl, Pasadena (94,194)

BRAZIL (0) 0
V
ITALY (0) 0
(0-0 After extra time Brazil won 3-2 on penalties)

TOTAL ATTENDANCE
3,587,538 over 52 matches (Average 68,991)

TOP GOALSCORERS (6 GOALS EACH)
Oleg Salenko, Russia & Hristo Stoichkov, Bulgaria

"SOMEBODY RECENTLY TOLD ME THAT DR. HENRY KISSINGER WAS IN THE LOCKER ROOM BEFORE THE GAME AND I HAD COMPLETELY BLANKED THAT OUT. I NEVER REMEMBERED THAT, AND ONCE I WAS REMINDED OF IT I SAID: 'OH, MY GOSH, IT'S TRUE'. I ONLY SAY THAT TO ILLUSTRATE THAT IT WAS SURREAL."

Alexi Lalas, US defender

INTRODUCTION

The first World Cup not hosted in either Europe or South America controversially went to the USA, which was not known for its football fervour and one where there was no domestic professional league at the time. Football came a long way down the pecking order in a country where the four dominant sports are not exactly international in their scope. Although in light of some of the recent decisions on selecting hosts, such as giving Qatar the 2022 tournament, this was a great deal more rational and understandable.

This was the first World Cup in which three points were awarded for a win a move intended to encourage teams to take the risk of winning and it seemed fitting it happened in the US, as the idea of a draw is anathema to their sporting culture. For the same reason it was the right place for the first World Cup to be decided on penalties. And lest we forget there were the buggies, which carted the injured off the pitch and straight on to the golf course by the look of it.

FIFA would point to the popularity of what was by far and away the best attended World Cup as justification for choosing the States. Football might not have had such a strong, well-established presence in the US as in other parts of the world, but what it lacked in tradition it made up for with a strong infrastructure and excellent stadiums. There was no need for any large-scale construction projects and so they avoided the customary desperate race to finish new stadia in time.

That preparedness is something that many previous hosts lacked and it is doubtful that they could have coped with the number of people attending as more than 3.5 million flocked to the nine stadiums spread across the country. This impressive aggregate attendance was achieved with only 52 matches and although there have been 64 matches played since 1998 no other tournament has come close to topping the figures achieved in 1994. The average crowd of just under 69,000 is remarkable, with the next highest being nearly 53,000 in Germany in 2006. Nobody could accuse the Americans of not embracing the tournament with unbound enthusiasm and gusto.

As ever, the Americans were keen to make a song and dance about being host and what the opening ceremony lacked in subtlety it made up for in complexity and the odd mishap. Oprah Winfrey was an interesting choice as the master of ceremonies and when she fell off the stage while introducing Diana Ross it seemed set to be the lasting image. However, that was soon eclipsed by Ross' attempt to score a 'penalty'. The goalkeeper obligingly dived out of the way but comically the singer put her shot wide. Four weeks later one of the world's greatest players would follow in Ross' footsteps, from the Supreme to the ridiculous.

The record for individual scoring in a single match was set by Oleg Salenko who scored five goals in less than an hour during the Russians' 6-1 demolition of Cameroon. Salenko only scored one other goal in the remainder of the games but still managed to share the Golden Boot with Hristo Stoichkov. But Salenko's extraordinary achievement was overshadowed by the consolation Cameroonian goal as it was scored by Roger Milla who thus became the oldest goal scorer at a World Cup at just over 42. Salenko must be a little miffed that this was what would be remembered rather than his own individual goal tally.

Any record of the 1994 World Cup cannot ignore the tragic murder of Andres Escobar. His own goal (ironically the only own goal of the tournament) against USA received the harshest punishment imaginable as he was gunned down a few weeks later in Medellín. Whether this was directly as a result of his slip is open to conjecture but most people make the connection. A driver for one of the drug cartels was convicted of his murder but some 24 years later, in January 2018 drug lord Santiago Henao was charged with his murder and is now awaiting trial. Henao's conviction may finally bring a sense of closure to this tragic episode.

DEBUTANTS

Considering the fanaticism that characterises their club football it was somewhat of a surprise that Greece had not qualified before 1994. Their initial stab was one of the weaker efforts, scoring none while leaking 10 goals in their three matches, although there were extenuating circumstances. They were in a tough group with Argentina, who had reached the previous two finals, and Bulgaria who had knocked out France in their qualifying group and would arguably become the team of the tournament by beating Germany in the last eight on their way to the semi-finals. Greece never really recovered from their 4-0 loss to Argentina but all the media focus after that match was directed towards Maradona and his crazed goal celebration which saw him get up close and personal to the camera. What at first appeared to be a release of pent-up emotion was shown to be something quite different by a failed drugs test after Argentina's next game against Nigeria, who were also making their debut.

The Africans, led by their twin strike force Rashidi Yekini and Daniel Amokachi, who both scored in their opening game, began the tournament with an impressive 3-0 win against the Bulgarians. This was the largest victory by a team in its first ever World Cup match in the post-War era so was a real feather in the Nigerians' cap. Despite losing to Argentina they topped the group on superior goal difference and were a few minutes away from beating Italy in the last-16 match, only to succumb to the eventual finalists in extra time courtesy of a Roberto Baggio brace. Again the African nations were making a statement that they very much belonged in this company.

The third country appearing for the first time were Saudi Arabia who performed creditably and could even lay claim to the goal of the tournament and one which had parallels with a similarly wonderful individual effort from 1986. The sight of a handful of Belgian defenders flailing in the wake of a dazzling run evoked memories of Maradona's solo effort in the semi-final in Mexico. Saeed Al-Owairan's goal could be considered even more impressive as he set off from his own half and then sliced through the heart of the Belgian defence before finishing adroitly into the roof of the net. Al-Owairan secured his name in the World Cup pantheon and helped Saudi Arabia make it through to the second round before they went out to Sweden.

Inevitably he earned the moniker 'Maradona of the Arabs' as well as a gift of a Rolls Royce on his return home. Just as the original Maradona departed in disgrace Al-Owairan's life followed a similar trajectory soon afterwards, encountering his own problems after his fifteen minutes of fame. His goal alerted a clutch of European clubs but he could not capitalise on all the attention as Saudis were banned from playing abroad. His frustration led to him falling by the wayside and after being caught in a red-light district in Cairo he was jailed and banned from playing. He was subsequently pardoned and made it to the 1998 World Cup but he never recaptured the form that had thrust him into the spotlight.

HOME NATIONS

After the high of reaching the semi-final in 1990, England repeated the low of their failures to reach the 1974 and 1978 tournaments, as Graham Taylor's men tripped up, finishing third in their qualifying group behind Norway and the Netherlands. There was much railing against the misfortune suffered against the Dutch at Wembley, including Jan Wouters' elbow into Paul Gascoigne's face going unpunished and Ronald Koeman escaping with a clear professional foul on David Platt. The reprieved Koeman's free-kick in Rotterdam twisted the knife into an England team that was as uninspiring as it was unfortunate. It should be remembered that the English also lost to the Norwegians and drew with the Poles so much of the damage was self-inflicted. England still had an outside chance in their final game, against San Marino. England needed Poland to beat the Dutch and at the same time win their own game by seven clear goals. England missed out as not only did they only secure a six goal winning margin but also Holland won. To add insult to injury San Marino's goal came after just 8.3 seconds, which at the time was the fastest goal in World Cup qualifying history.

After their humiliation at the hands of Gaetjans et al in 1950 the English could be forgiven for not being especially enamoured by any World Cup connections with the USA.

Scotland missed out for the first time since 1966. Although they were undefeated at home in qualifying, three away losses to Italy, Switzerland and Portugal proved fatal as they finished a distant fourth, as did both Wales and Northern Ireland. This was the first tournament since 1950 that had no representative from the United Kingdom and as a result many adopted the Republic of Ireland as their team as after all they did have an English manager and plenty of 'assimilated' players.

Ireland's opening game pitted them against Italy in the Giants stadium and appositely they performed a notable giant-killing when Ray Houghton's looping shot gave them an early lead that they defended manfully. This group could not have ended any tighter as all four teams finished on four points with an identical goal difference of zero and Norway were eliminated as they only scored one goal and Ireland made the cut having scored two.

RED MIST, RED CARDS & RED FACES

After the plethora of 16 red cards in 1990 there was one fewer in 1994 but the one that sticks in the mind came from the flying elbow of a Brazilian. In the second round game with the USA on Independence Day Leonardo and Tab Ramos were battling on the touchline when Leonardo decided he needed to assert his authority over the situation and swung his elbow full into the face of the American. It was as clear a red card as you are likely to see, however, one man somehow missed it and that happened to be Kevin Keegan who was on commentary with Alan Parry at the time.

Keegan told the television audience that he was not sure that it was deliberate: "I didn't think he had done that much wrong. He was being held. He was being fouled first." But after each successive showing and Parry's prompting the intention became clearer until even Keegan had to admit that is was a cold, calculated assault.

The force of the blow left Ramos with a fractured skull and he was hospitalised for three months. So much for that celebrated Samba style of the *Seleção*. This team was slightly different to its predecessors in that it was prosaic rather than poetic and had suffered the humiliation of being the first Brazilian side to lose a World Cup qualifier, to Bolivia. With the grizzled Dunga at the heart of the team, who was more in the mould of an Italian destroyer than a free creative spirit, there was something entirely appropriate about how they ground out victory in the stalemate of the only goalless final in World Cup history.

FOOTNOTE

When Diana Ross' farcical missed spot kick ushered in the tournament little did we know how central penalties would be to the next four weeks. The players had clearly learned from the singer's failure as all 15 penalties taken during regular time were converted—the only time there has been a 100% success rate—and it seemed the tournament was fated to end with the first penalty shoot-out in World Cup Final history. Sure enough after Brazil and Italy had cancelled each other out the teams headed for that most painful of endings for the Italians and Roberto Baggio in particular.

Baggio had been as instrumental in getting Italy to the final as he had been in getting them to the semi-final four years earlier. He scored five goals in the three knock-out matches and the stage was set for his crowning glory even though his movement was restricted by a hamstring injury and he had to wear heavy strapping during the final. Baggio was known for his exceptionally cool command of penalty-taking, he had a 100% record for the national side and a conversion rate of almost 90% in club football. If the Italians were to choose a player to take such a highly pressurised kick then Baggio was the man.

It was not to be, although he was not alone in missing his spot kick in the shoot-out, another Italian hero Franco Baresi and Daniele Massaro missed the first two. However, Baggio's was the crucial fifth that handed Brazil their fourth World Cup as he blasted it over the bar with uncharacteristic rashness. He did achieve some sort of redemption when he successfully converted his next World Cup penalty in Italy's opening game of the 1998 tournament, salvaging a late draw with Chile. Baggio wrote in his autobiography that he had "killed the ghost with that penalty," but that sounds like wishful thinking as that uncharacteristically un-Zen like Pasadena moment is the one that everyone remembers.

1998

HOST
France

CITIES
Bordeaux, Lens, Lyon, Marseille, Montpellier, Nantes, Paris, Saint Etienne, Toulouse

DEBUTANTS (4)
Croatia, Jamaica, Japan, South Africa

FINAL
Sunday 12 July, Stade de France (80,000)

BRAZIL (0) 0
V
FRANCE (2) 3
Zidane 2, Petit
(Half-time score in brackets)

TOTAL ATTENDANCE
2,785,100 over 64 matches (Average 43,517)

TOP GOALSCORER (6)
Davor Šuker, Croatia

"HE'S UNDER MORE PRESSURE THAN ANYONE ELSE IN THE WORLD, AND ALL THAT'S HAPPENED TODAY HAS LEFT HIM VERY DISTRESSED. I HAVE A WIFE, FAMILY AND CHILDREN TO GO HOME TO, BUT HE DOESN'T HAVE THAT. RONALDO DOESN'T HAVE THE SUPPORT YOU NEED. I URGE EVERYONE TO JUST LEAVE THE BOY ALONE."

Roberto Carlos, Ronaldo's room-mate who discovered him having a seizure before the World Cup final.

INTRODUCTION

This was the sixth and, as of the time of writing, last time a host nation won the World Cup. The French team peaked at the right time as their midfield of Zinedine Zidane, Emmanuel Petit, Didier Deschamps, Youri Djorkaeff and Christian Karembeu were the strongest since that formidable team of 1982 who were so cruelly denied. Deschamps, harshly but perhaps justifiably nicknamed the 'water carrier' by Eric Cantona, and Karembeu provided the shield in front of the back four allowing Zidane, Petit and Djorkaeff to burst forward with a certain amount of freedom.

After jettisoning both Cantona and David Ginola, French manager Aimé Jacquet struggled to find a focal point for his side's attack, which was mildly ironic considering the goal scoring exploits of Just Fontaine 40 years earlier. Thierry Henry was top scorer with just three goals and three other players—Zidane, Petit and the unlikeliest of all, Lilian Thuram— contributed two goals each. Thuram's pair were his only goals for France. They came in the same game - the semi-final against Croatia - and were separated by just 21 minutes. In his other 141 international appearances, which amounted to 210 hours on the pitch, he didn't score again.

Only one other country has won the World Cup without a player scoring at least four goals and that was Italy in 2006. Their scoring duties were shared between 10 players, eight of who scored once and two, Materazzi and Luca Toni, who scored twice each.

In the second round, French defender Laurent Blanc scored the first ever World Cup golden goal in the 113th minute against Paraguay. This proved to be a short-lived experiment as the golden goals rule was abandoned by FIFA after only one more tournament in 2002. The idea was good as it was intended to encourage teams to press for the decisive goal, however it had the opposite effect as teams retrenched scared of conceding. As so often fear of losing outweighs the desire to win. The other new rule implemented was the outlawing of the tackle from behind, which from this point on would be punished with a red card.

One would have expected a few red cards in the game between Iran and the USA, which was described with customary hyperbole by the President of the US Federation as 'the mother of all games'. The tension had been ratcheted up before the game with talk of protests and disruption, which ultimately did not materialise, but the fires were really stoked by the showing of a controversial film depicting the harsh conditions of life in post-revolution Iran on French television in the build-up to the match.

Despite all this background noise there was a rare showing of unity between the two sets of players in the pre-match formalities, which culminated in a joint team photograph. It was also significant that the Iranian coach Jalal Talebi had spent some of his formative career in California. The match itself passed without any incident and the fact that Iran went on to win was received with wild acclaim back home as politics for once was submerged beneath the delight that football can bring. As Talebi said just before the match: "Please don't make it too big for us. This is a game. A game."

DEBUTANTS

It is always refreshing to see new countries doing well and Croatia continued the pattern of debutants making a positive impression by securing third place. More notably they annihilated Germany in the quarter-finals in what was the *Die Mannschaft's* worst ever result in the latter stages of the competition and what turned out to be Lothar Matthäus' 25th and last World Cup appearance. Just after half time in their semi-final, Croatia even had the temerity to take the lead against the hosts France, but they could not hold on for what would have been a remarkable result.

Like Denmark in 1986, their kit with its bold red and white squares produced a striking look that drew similar admiring glances to their enterprising football. Davor Šuker was the tournament's leading scorer with six goals, which serendipitously was the sixth successive time that the Golden Boot had been won by a player scoring six goals. It was only the second time since 1934 that the top goal scorer was playing for a country that was appearing for the first time (Eusebio having achieved the same feat in 1966).

Oddly Croatia ended up in a group with two of the other three debutants: Japan and Jamaica. The Reggae Boyz were managed by Brazillian René Simões and he assembled a fair smattering of players from English clubs, such as Robbie Earle and Frank Sinclair who provided experience of playing at the top level. The Jamaicans bounced back from heavy defeats to both Croatia and Argentina in their first two matches to defeat Japan in their last game thanks to two Theodore Whitmore goals.

South Africa completed the quartet of new boys and they were also one of five African teams, the most that had appeared at a World Cup at that time. Bafana Bafana acquitted themselves pretty well after a tricky first match against the hosts, which ended in a 3-0 defeat. They then drew their next two games, with Benni McCarthy registering their first World Cup goal against Denmark, only for him to be outdone by Shaun Bartlett who scored twice as they drew with Saudi Arabia in their final group game.

HOME NATIONS

England returned to the fray, having secured qualification with a battling draw in Rome, characterised by Paul Ince's bandaged and bloody head. The ugly side of England's bulldog spirit unfortunately reared its head in France when fans fought running battles with both Tunisians and locals in Marseille to give another reminder of the 'English Disease'. The team progressed without too much trouble to the next round despite a hiccup in the second game against Romania when Graham Le Saux's injudicious challenge on his Chelsea team-mate Dan Petrescu led to a penalty from which the Romanians grabbed the winner. England's equaliser in that game came from Michael Owen who became the youngest English goal scorer at a World Cup aged just 18 and the only teenager to do so for the Three Lions.

The defeat to Romania meant that England faced Argentina, their nemesis of 12 years before, in the last 16. Naturally the game was a highly charged affair, which may go to explaining why there were two penalties in the first 10 minutes. Gabriel Batistuta opened the scoring for Argentina before Alan Shearer equalised. Six minutes later Michael Owen scored an extraordinary goal using his searing pace to burn past the Argentina defenders before finishing with composure. It ranks among the greatest scored by a teenager but in that moment Owen showed the advantages of youth when coupled with maturity. That was as good as it got for England. The frustration of conceding an equaliser on the stroke of half-time was exacerbated by the dismissal of David Beckham for a petulant kick at Diego Simeone. England paid the price for his immaturity when they lost the penalty shoot-out, having survived for 75 minutes a man short.

Scotland came through a tough qualification group that included Sweden and Austria. The most notable game was a non-event in Tallin. The Estonians took umbrage at the Scots' complaints about the floodlights which saw the kick-off moved forward. However, the home team did not turn up for the rearranged time leading to the bizarre sight of Scotland kicking off against nobody and the game being abandoned after three seconds. The re-match ended in a goalless draw and barely contained as much excitement.

In France Scotland had the misfortune to be paired with Brazil again and lost to a Tom Boyd own goal in the opening match of the tournament. It was a respectable result and performance, which they followed up with a draw against Norway. So it was all down to the last game against the weakest team in the group, Morocco. But Scotland did what only they can do and failed, miserably, losing 3-0 to the North Africans. This was their eighth World Cup and they still had not managed to progress to the second round. No other country has been to so many World Cups and failed to go beyond the first round. Worse still, since France they have failed five times in a row to even get to the finals, their longest ever absence.

RED CARDS & RED MIST

France are not known as an aggressive team but in this World Cup they managed to rack up more red cards than any other host country before or since. This was not the natural insouciance we expect from our Gallic neighbours. For such a naturally talented player Zidane certainly had a short fuse and was sent off a dozen times throughout his career. As the French were coasting to a 4-0 victory over Saudi Arabia Zidane showed his malevolent side, stamping on Fuad Amin and in what was not exactly a high stakes game it seemed a ridiculous act. In 2006 Zidane completed his own dirty double when he was sent off in the final after his 'chest butt' on Materazzi.

The other two French red cards came in the semi-final, when Blanc clashed with Slaven Bilić, and the final, when Marcel Desailly lost his legendary coolness and received a second booking for a ridiculous lunge on the halfway line. Thus France became the only World Cup winners to have a player sent off in both the semi-final and final. Not so much Allez les Bleus as Allez les Rouges, maybe.

The newly expanded tournament set a high for red cards with 22 dismissals in 64 matches, which is going at quite a lick. Cameroon collected three red cards in France and when Rigobert Song received his second yellow card early in the second half against Chile he became the first player to be sent off in two different tournaments, having been sent off against Brazil in 1994.

Keeping it in the family, his nephew Alex was dismissed in 2014, thus completing a unique if unwanted Song hat-trick.

FOOTNOTE

Following their victory over England the Romanians decided in their infinite wisdom to leave a lasting impression on the global audience by all having a blonde rinse. The reason given was that it would somehow bring the team good fortune. However, considering in their next match they scraped a draw with Tunisia and then lost to Croatia in the last 16 it clearly did not work. The sight of a great player like Gheorghe Hagi looking like a backing singer for Madonna was enough to make you weep.

Such a stylistic realignment would certainly have challenged the Argentinian squad whose manager, the former World Cup winning captain Daniel Passarella, was somewhat of a stickler for conformity. In the wake of Maradona's downfall in 1994 Passarella was determined to draw a strong disciplinary line and so prior to the tournament he set out some pretty draconian rules, which included the banning of earrings, long hair and homosexuals. One of the squad's better players Fernando Redondo, who was playing at Real Madrid, was told to get his flowing locks shorn if he wanted to be considered for inclusion. Redondo refused and was left out of the World Cup squad with Passarella refusing to back down.

Claudio Caniggia also fell foul of Passarella's hard line and Gabriel Batistuta was sidelined for most of the qualifying campaign, but Passarella did relent when faced with the possibility of losing his main striker in the tournament itself. Ultimately the manager's disciplinarian attitude bowed to expediency as he realised leaving out his main source of goals would be damaging to the the team's prospects. Batistuta had scored half of Argentina's goals in 1994 including a hat-trick against Greece. So when he notched a hat-trick against Jamaica in the group game he became the only player to score hat-tricks in two World Cups, again being responsible for half of Argentina's goals. He is also one of the select few players who have scored in three different tournaments. He scored just once in Japan/South Korea but he still scored half the team's goals for the third successive time as Argentina went out at the group stage for the first time since 1962.

HOST
Japan & South Korea

CITIES
Japan: Ibaraki, Kobe, Niigata, Oita, Osaka, Rifu,
Saitama, Sapporo, Shizuoka, Yokohama

S.Korea; Busan, Daegu, Daejon, Gwanju,
Incheon, Jeju, Jeonju, Seoul, Suwon, Ulan

DEBUTANTS (4)
China, Ecuador, Senegal, Slovenia

FINAL
Sunday 30 June, International Stadium, Yokohama (69,029)

BRAZIL (0) 2
Ronaldo 2
V
GERMANY (0) 0
(Half-time score in brackets)

TOTAL ATTENDANCE
2,705,134 over 64 matches (Average 42,268)

TOP GOALSCORER (8)
Ronaldo, Brazil

"I DON'T UNDERSTAND WHY THEY DID THIS TO ME. EVEN NOW, I CANNOT FIND ANY REASON TO CONVINCE MYSELF, I STILL CANNOT ACCEPT IT. WHEN I SCORED THAT GOAL, THE FEELING WAS UNBELIEVABLE. IT WAS THE BEST MOMENT OF MY CAREER."

Ahn Jung-Hwan, scorer of South Korea's 'golden goal'
against Italy, talks about being sacked by Perugia.

INTRODUCTION

2002 was the only time that the World Cup has been co-hosted and although logistically everything ran smoothly FIFA has publicly declared that this idea will not be repeated. As a result of two countries sharing the World Cup the 20 cities used to stage games was higher than the usual 12. Of those 20 all but two had to have new stadia built from scratch but there were no issues with missing deadlines.

Despite the generous spread of cities, the Japanese capital, Tokyo was not used and nor was the city of Toyota, which spent $40m building a 40,000 capacity stadium against the wishes of many of its residents, only to be overlooked because the stadium in Niigata boasted better transport links. So it was not used at all during the World Cup and eventually became home to Nagoya Grampus 8, which once upon a time was Gary Lineker's club.

Not everything was harmonious between the two hosts and it was inevitable that there would be some tension considering the Japanese had ruled South Korea between 1910 and 1945. The South Koreans viewed the Japanese as opportunists, even ingénues, and not a true football nation as they had only qualified once before in 1998 whereas the Koreans could justifiably claim some pedigree as this was their sixth World Cup appearance, although they had never progressed beyond the first round in any of the previous five.

All that was about to change, to the delight of their animated, red-shirted fans South Korea topped their group and finally at the sixth attempt they had made it to the second round, alongside Japan. Although Japan faltered at the last 16 stage, the Koreans surpassed their wildest dreams by making it not just to the quarter-finals but all the way to the semi-finals. When they beat Italy in the last 16 thanks to Ahn Jung-Hwan's golden goal the victory had clear parallels with neighbours North Korea's triumph over the same opponents in 1966. The result was clearly too much for Ahn's Italian club Perugia, whose president showed a remarkable lack of grace by announcing that he was terminating the Korean striker's loan deal and that the player would no longer be welcome at the club. Thus Ahn possibly became the only player to be sacked for scoring a goal.

South Korea then took on another European giant Spain in the quarter finals and went through on penalties after a goalless draw. Just one match away from the final they were in uncharted territory for an Asian country, having beaten four European countries along the way (they overcame Portugal and Poland in their group). Like the Italians, the Spaniards did not take to losing with good grace and there were heavy insinuations of bias towards the co-hosts. Even though there had been some debatable decisions, there was nothing out of the ordinary and to infer it was more than just bad judgment from the officials is surely wide of the mark. Despite this carping the South Koreans had done themselves proud and Ahn quite rightly turned down Perugia's later attempts to re-sign him having reversed their original decision and he found another club, this time in Japan.

DEBUTANTS

As this was the first time the tournament had been held in Asia it was a case of perfect timing for China to finally qualify. Having waited so long you might have thought the World Cup gods would be kind to the world's most populous nation in the draw but this was not the case and they were thrust into a group with the teams which would ultimately finish first and third, Brazil and Turkey respectively. Costa Rica were also a decent side and only missed out on qualifying on goal difference to Turkey. Although China had opted for the experienced, steady hands of Bora Milutinović as their coach they failed to score and conceded nine goals in their three matches. Their time will surely come.

By contrast to the 1.4 billion Chinese, Slovenia has a population of just over two million and became one of the smallest countries to play in the World Cup. Considering their size they certainly punched above their weight and at least managed to score in their three defeats. Meanwhile Ecuador surprised the Croatians in their last group game and managed to beat the team that had created such a stir in France, but they still ended bottom of their group.

The real upstarts were Senegal who, like the Cameroonians in 1990, rattled the cage of the previous World Cup winners in the opening game as they beat a lacklustre France 1-0 through a Papa Bouba Diop goal. This was the start of an incredible implosion from the 1998 champions that ended in a tame surrender of their title. Senegal were naturally cock-a-hoop with their start, having beaten their former colonial masters but they did not rest on their laurels and made sure of qualifying for the second round with draws against Denmark and Uruguay in their other group games.

The Senegalese did not stop there, beating Sweden in the last 16 thanks to a golden goal from Henri Camara, his second strike of the game. In the following match the golden goal went against them as Turkey progressed to the semi-finals. This was to be the last golden goal to be scored in the World Cup and it left Senegal as the second African team to reach the last eight of the World Cup.

HOME NATIONS

England were again the sole representatives from the UK but they still conspired to qualify the hard way. A dismal start to their campaign saw them lose to Germany in the last ever game at the old Wembley stadium, a result that led to Kevin Keegan's resignation. This was followed by a goalless draw in Finland, which left England bottom of the group and five points adrift of leaders Germany. Keegan was soon replaced by Sven-Göran Eriksson, the first foreigner to manage the England team and slowly they reeled the Germans in before destroying them 5-1 in the penultimate game in Munich, courtesy of a Michael Owen hat-trick. Thus England went into their final game against Greece top of the group on goal difference and all they had to do was match or better Germany's final result. What could possibly go wrong? After all in seven previous games against Greece, England had won six - including a comfortable 2-0 win in Athens four months earlier - and drawn one.

There was a shock in store at Old Trafford as England spluttered and stuttered. They went behind twice and were trailing in stoppage time, while the Germans were playing out a draw against Finland. Only David Beckham seemed remotely aware that disaster was looming and not only did he score a last-gasp free-kick to rescue the team, it should be remembered that he had been everywhere throughout the match displaying an urgency that his team-mates were sadly lacking. So reliant had the team become on one player that there was a national meltdown when Beckham fractured his metatarsal a few months prior to the start of the tournament.

Beckham did recover in time for the tournament and it was just as well as he scored the decisive penalty in a 1-0 win against Argentina. The goal made amends for previous failings and helped England limp through their group after a 1-1 draw with Sweden and a particularly uninspiring goalless stalemate with Nigeria. They seemed to wake up for the last 16 as they dismissed Denmark 3-0 to set up a quarter-final clash with Brazil. Seemingly the whole nation woke up early to see if Beckham could drag England any further. Owen gave England the lead but Rivaldo brought Brazil level on the stroke of halftime. Five minutes into the second half Ronaldinho gave Brazil the lead through a long-range free-kick that floated past a nonplussed David Seaman. A few minutes later he was sent off giving England more than half an hour to try and break down 10 men, but the eventual champions survived without too much trouble.

To be knocked out before 9am UK time seemed especially cruel as the whole day stretched out ahead of us and the novelty of having a hangover whilst morosely eating a couple of slices of toast wore off pretty quickly. And so we were left to contemplate how England's 50th finals match had panned out as a microcosm of the World Cup experience. The hopes raised by Owen's opening goal, the tension of trying to hold on to the lead, the disappointment of conceding the equaliser just before half-time and then the outrageous nature of the second goal before hope was rekindled by Ronaldinho's dismissal only for it to end in frustration and recriminations. Such is the lot of the England supporter.

RED MIST & RED FACES

The Dutch and the French had proved to be the masters of self-destruction in previous tournaments with a penchant for internal squabbles, hissy fits, spectacular fallouts and a capacity to pick a fight with anyone about anything just for the sake of it. This affinity to disunity would normally have been anathema to the Republic of Ireland, who may not have had the most gifted players but more than made up for that with a gritty togetherness of spirit that served them so well in 1990 and 1994. Jack Charlton made a virtue of their underdog status that had taken them to the quarter-finals and the last 16 in their previous appearances.

So what happened in 2002 and in particular in Saipan was a colossal shock to the whole ethos of the team and the solid foundations that Jack built. It was always going to be a tough task to follow in Charlton's footsteps and Mick McCarthy, the man entrusted to do so in 1996, initially struggled to match the feats of his predecessor. Ireland failed to qualify for 1998 World Cup and the Euros in 2000 so there was some relief that they squeezed into the 2002 via a play-off win against Iran.

Unfortunately for McCarthy the Irish FA's preparations for the tournament were not the best and certainly not to the liking of Roy Keane who took exception to the amateurish approach and confronted the manager in the ballroom of the team hotel in front of the rest of the squad. Keane's infamous rant is now part of Irish folklore and is always worth repeating for its brutal ferocity. "Mick, you're a liar... you're a fucking wanker. I didn't rate you as a player, I don't rate you as a manager, and I don't rate you as a person. You're a fucking wanker and you can stick your World Cup up your arse. The only reason I have any dealings with you is that somehow you are the manager of my country! You can stick it up your bollocks."

It was not exactly Oscar Wilde but what it lacked in subtlety it more than compensated for with clarity and a sense of purpose. As soon as he had finished his diatribe Keane was homeward bound and the Irish were light of pretty much their only recognised world-class player. Despite this turmoil and Keane's subsequent absence, the Irish did maintain their 100% record of making it through to the second round, only to lose out to the Spanish in a penalty shoot-out. Affairs came full circle a few years later when McCarthy took over at Ipswich in 2012. One of his main tasks was to clear up the mess left after the disastrous 20-month reign of one of his predecessors at Portman Road, of course none other than Roy Keane.

FOOTNOTE

As far as defences of the trophy are concerned France's lamentable performance in 2002 must be considered the most feeble of all. The French arrived in Japan/Korea in fine fettle. They had added the European Championship and the Confederations Cup to their home World Cup triumph, so were in possession of a unique international football treble. They also had an improved squad as it contained forwards who could score goals, Sylvain Wiltord and David Trezeguet were infinitely more preferable to the previous pairing of Stéphane Guivarc'h or Christophe Dugarry.

Zidane warmed up for the tournament with an incredible goal for Real Madrid in the Champions League final so everything was rosy in the French garden. Unfortunately things began to unravel when Zidane got injured in a friendly with South Korea and then got worse with the opening defeat to Senegal. Thierry Henry's red card in the second match with Uruguay hinted at the problems being encountered by the champions. Their final group game against Denmark did not provide the necessary reprieve and the French were sent packing, bottom of the group, goalless and vanquished.

2006

HOST
Germany

CITIES
Berlin, Cologne, Dortmund, Frankfurt, Gelsenkirchen, Hamburg, Hanover, Kaiserslautern, Leipzig, Munich, Nuremberg, Stuttgart

DEBUTANTS (6)
Angola, Ghana, Ivory Coast, Togo, Trinidad & Tobago, Ukraine

FINAL
Sunday 9 July, Olympiastadion, Berlin (69,000)

FRANCE (1) 1
Zidane
V
ITALY (1) 1
Materazzi
(1-1 After extra time, Italy won 5-3 on penalties)

TOTAL ATTENDANCE
3,359,424 over 64 matches (Average 52,491)

TOP GOALSCORER (5)
Miroslav Klose, Germany

"IT WAS SEEN BY TWO OR THREE BILLION PEOPLE ON TELEVISION AND MILLIONS AND MILLIONS OF CHILDREN WERE WATCHING. IT WAS AN INEXCUSABLE GESTURE AND TO THEM, AND THE PEOPLE IN EDUCATION WHOSE JOB IT IS TO SHOW CHILDREN WHAT THEY SHOULD AND SHOULDN'T DO, I WANT TO APOLOGISE."

Zinedine Zidane shows his contrition for his chest butt on Marco Materazzi in the Final.

INTRODUCTION

This was a very different Germany to the one that hosted the 1974 Finals when East Germany made their one and only appearance. The unified nation, which included the former East German city of Leipzig as one of the venues, made a concerted effort to make all the fans welcome. It was also significant that the Germans were now proud of their flag after many years in which they were slightly sheepish and ashamed of any association with nationalism.

The introduction of fan parks by FIFA is certainly one of those rare initiatives of which they can be proud as it allowed thousands of people to watch the game en masse without having tickets. Having proved to be a great success these parks are now very much considered an integral part of major tournaments and are here to stay. The vast majority of the supporters who spent time in Germany basked in the relaxed atmosphere, the excellent transport links and were full of praise for the welcoming hosts. Indeed I can attest to that convivial environment as I travelled to Nuremberg for England's game with Trinidad & Tobago. A thoroughly enjoyable experience but a crap match.

DEBUTANTS

This was the highest number of debutants since the second tournament back in 1934. Of the six, four were from Africa. Just like Senegal in 1998 Angola were fated to meet their former colonial masters, Portugal, in their first match. Eight of the Angolan players were at Portuguese clubs and they gave the opposition a decent run for their money despite conceding an early goal. A couple of draws against Mexico and Iran were not enough to get them through to the next round.

Ivory Coast were expected to do well with a strong squad and some familiar names to British audiences, including Didier Drogba and the Touré brothers, Kolo and Yaya. However, they were drawn in a very tough group including Argentina, the Netherlands plus Serbia and Montenegro. Losing to both the strongest teams was disappointing but not surprising, however they secured a victory in a thrilling match against Serbia and Montenegro, fighting back from two goals down to win even without their main man Drogba.

Ghana made their presence felt after an opening defeat to Italy as they beat both Czech Republic and USA to progress to the second round where they met a Brazilian team who were just hitting their stride and went down 3-0. Perhaps the real story came from by far the smallest African country at the Finals. With a population of only seven million Togo, who had not been close to qualification before, were led by the mercurial Emmanuel Adebayor so they arrived in Germany with a semblance of hope. That hope was pretty much extinguished when their coach Otto Pfister fell out with Adebayor (not an unusual occurrence) and others over bonuses and resigned in the week before their opening game. Although Pfister then performed a sharp U-turn on the eve of their match with South Korea, this less than ideal preparation led to Togo losing all their games.

Players from Ukraine had appeared at previous World Cups as part of the Soviet Union team but this was the county's first appearance since it had gained independence. The team was captained by Andriy Shevchenko, who had established himself in the European elite during seven years at AC Milan in which time he was voted European Player of the Year in 2004. He joined Chelsea straight after the tournament. They had a bruising introduction to the World Cup when Spain, led by David Villa in sparkling form alongside his strike partner Fernando Torres, made light work of them with a 4-0 win.

Ukraine recovered their equilibrium with an equally convincing win over the Saudis and a Shevchenko penalty took care of Tunisia, securing their passage into the second round, where they met Switzerland. After a goalless 120 minutes the penalty shoot-out made history as the Swiss contrived to miss all three of theirs and thus became the only team to not register in a World Cup penalty shoot-out. They also became the only team eliminated without conceding a goal but that consolation was buried beneath the feebleness of their penalties. Ukraine looked like the team more accustomed to this sort of pressure. They were unruffled by their talisman Shevchenko missing their first penalty and converted the next three. This set up a quarter-final tie against Italy, a dream for Shevchenko. "It's very special for me after playing and living for so many years in Milan," he said in the build up to the game. "I have many friends in Italy and Italian football after playing all those years." However, Italy ruined the dream with a 3-0 win as Luca Toni's muscularity proved too much for the Ukrainians.

But of the half dozen first-timers the sheer delight that greeted Trinidad and Tobago's qualification will take some beating. After their play-off win against Bahrain their prime minister Patrick Manning declared a national holiday to celebrate the achievement by the smallest country to ever qualify (up until Iceland in 2018). There was more reason to party when they drew their opening game against Sweden even though they were a man light for most of the second half. And so next up, the country that they gained independence from in 1962, England. England's tortuous win by two late goals from Peter Crouch and Steven Gerrard could not dampen the enthusiasm of the Soca Warriors. Leaving the ground I distinctly remember the contrast in moods between the English who were morose and taciturn whereas the Caribbean mood was uplifting and joyous. It felt rather confusing to witness how differently the winners and the losers reacted.

HOME NATIONS

Again England were the sole British participants. Their qualification was not nearly as tight or streaky as in 2002, beating their only genuine challengers, Poland in their last game to top the group. At the tournament proper a narrow win over Paraguay thanks to a Carlos Gamarra own goal preceded the Trinidad and Tobago match. By the time England met Sweden, qualification was assured. An entertaining 2-2 draw, which featured Joe Cole's finest moment in an England shirt, the 2,000th World Cup goal scored by Marcus Allbäck and a last-minute equaliser by Henrik Larsson, meant England topped the group.

A second round match against Ecuador was settled by an early Beckham free-kick but in none of their games had the Three Lions looked particularly convincing. England fans and players alike will have had a feeling of déjà vu after quarter final defeat to Portugal. Yet again England had a key man sent off, this time it was Wayne Rooney, and hung on until the end of extra time. Yet again they crashed out on penalties. So for the third time in four World Cups England lost in a shoot-out and after Italy went on to win the final against France on penalties they were left as the only team to have been involved in three World Cup shoot-outs and lost them all.

RED CARD & RED MIST

In stark contrast to the warm hospitality off the pitch there was more than a fair share of aggression and antagonism on the pitch. The total of 28 red cards is the highest in any World Cup. An average of close to one sending-off every two matches was pretty staggering with one game standing out like a particularly sore thumb. The last-16 tie between Portugal and the Netherlands, two teams that one would not normally associate with the dark arts, set all sorts of unwanted records. This game racked up a staggering total of 20 cards—four reds and 16 yellows—which is an average of one card every four and a half minutes, which didn't leave much room for football.

Following in the footsteps of previous pugilistic encounters and dubbed inevitably as The Battle of Nuremberg, this was a game that made grown men wince. The tone was established as early as the second minute when Mark van Bommel picked up the first yellow card for letting Cristiano Ronaldo know he was there by unceremoniously tripping him up. His team-mate Khalid Boulahrouz quickly followed him into the referee's book in the eighth minute. His brutal stamp on Ronaldo's thigh left the Portuguese limping and eventually he succumbed to the injury and was substituted shortly after the half hour mark. Even before his departure Portugal had evened up the bookings tally and on it went. Among the cynical tackling there was a sprinkling of diving and feigned injuries littered throughout the match.

Just after the 30-minute mark Costinha was booked for hacking down Phillip Cocu and in first-half injury time he received a second for as deliberate a handball as you are ever likely to see, duly picking up the game's first red card. The first half was relatively tame compared to the second 45 minutes as both sides upped the ante. Within the space of just over 15 minutes nine players were booked including second yellows for both Boulahrouz and Deco, whose first had only came five minutes before. Luis Figo was fortunate to receive just a yellow after he sneaked in a retaliatory head-butt on Van Bommel. Figo's manager Luiz Felipe Scolari defended his action, saying: "Jesus Christ was able to turn the other cheek but Luis Figo isn't Jesus Christ." Added to this almost biblical storm there were a couple of good old-fashioned melees with plenty of pushing and shoving and more besides as players either went down like flies or were ordered from the pitch.

The Russian referee Valentin Ivanov, who was appropriately dressed in a bright yellow shirt, could have been guilty of being a little too liberal in handing out his cards from the outset but then again he missed quite a few incidents that would have normally been punished so the culpability lay firmly with the players.

To round it all off, well into added time Giovanni van Bronckhorst joined the ever-lengthening queue for the early ablutions with his second yellow for fouling Tiago. Rumours that Ivanov has suffered from RSI ever since have never been verified. Just to let you know Portugal won the game 1-0.

FOOTNOTE

If ever a player deserved a fitting goodbye to the international stage it was Zinedine Zidane. He had graced the 1998 Finals and delivered the hosts the World Cup with his pair of headed goals. After the blip of 2002, 2006 seemed to be the perfect denouement for one of the classiest players of the previous decade. The final started as the script demanded with Zidane opening the scoring early from the penalty spot. That was only the second goal that Italy had conceded in the whole tournament, the other being an own goal. So alongside France in 1998 and Spain in 2010 Italy hold the joint record for the lowest number of goals conceded.

But within 12 minutes Zidane's *bête noir* Materazzi equalised. The Italian defender had returned from suspension in the semi-final having been sent off against Australia in the last 16. The goal scorers were then embroiled in the defining moment of the match, if not the tournament, with 10 minutes of extra time remaining when a clearly riled Zidane infamously floored the Italian centre back with a head butt to the chest. The image of Zidane peeling off his sweat bands in sorry resignation at his stupidity and its inevitable conclusion will live long in the memory. Zidane would undoubtedly have taken one of the resulting penalties and probably scored but it was Materazzi who stepped up confidently to convert Italy's second while David Trezeguet crucially missed for France. Ironically, the day after the final Zidane was awarded the player of the tournament award.

2010

HOST
South Africa

CITIES
Bloemfentein, Cape Town, Durban, Johannesburg, Nelspruit, Phokeng, Polokwane, Port Elizabeth, Pretoria

DEBUTANTS (1)
Slovakia

FINAL
Sunday 11 July, First National Bank Stadium, Johannesburg (84,490)

THE NETHERLANDS (0) 0 0
V
SPAIN (0) 0 1
Iniesta
(After extra time)

TOTAL ATTENDANCE
3,178,856 over 64 matches (Average 49,670)

TOP GOALSCORERS (5 GOALS EACH)
Thomas Müller, Germany
Diego Forlán, Uruguay
Wesley Sneijder, Netherlands
David Villa, Spain

"FOOTBALL GIVES EMOTIONS IN THIS DERANGED WORLD. LOOK AT THE NEWS AND YOU SEE THE WORLD APPEARS TO HAVE SUDDENLY STOPPED AND THE TV CAMERAS WILL AFTER JULY 12 BE USED EVERYWHERE IN THE WORLD. WE ARE GIVING HOPE TO THE WORLD THAT PERHAPS THROUGH FOOTBALL WE CAN BECOME BETTER HUMAN BEINGS."

A dewy-eyed Sepp Blatter on the impact of the World Cup.

INTRODUCTION

And so the World Cup road show finally arrived in Africa as FIFA's aim of spreading their patronage across the globe paved the way for South Africa to be the continent's first host. There were concerns expressed that there would be issues with safety because of the high levels of crime particularly in the main cities of Johannesburg and Cape Town. South Africa's reputation certainly suffered in comparison with the smooth, safe running of the 2006 tournament in Germany. In the end those fears were generally unfounded and there was more angst over the irregular flight of the official Adidas ball and the blaring plastic horns used by the fans.

The Jabulani ball was introduced with the usual hoopla associated with the new design. Jabulani means 'to celebrate' in Zulu but there was not much celebrating by those who were most directly affected and it actually became a cause célèbre for goalkeepers who complained bitterly about the unusual, exaggerated trajectory.

Adidas's revolutionary 'grip and groove' technology that was supposed to ensure the perfect roundness and improved aerodynamics did not make the grade. The players, led by keepers including Julio Cesar, Gianluigi Buffon, Iker Casillas and Claudio Bravo were unconvinced and did not hold back in their criticism. It was compared to a beach-ball and a supermarket ball and England keeper David James weighed in with these prophetic words: "The ball is dreadful. There are undoubtedly going to be some goals scored in this tournament which in previous tournaments with different balls would not have been scored. It will allow some people to score extra goals, but leave some goalkeepers looking daft." Just ask James' team-mate Robert Green, who tried to mask his ineptitude in the opening match by blaming the unpredictability of the Jabulani's flight.

If unpredictable balls were not bad enough we then had to face up to the constant background noise created by vuvuzelas. I distinctly remember watching the first game from South Africa and on hearing the noise for the first time I was wondering how a swarm of bees could make such a commotion. It became the soundtrack of the tournament but it soon moved from being a curiosity into a full-blown nuisance, a particularly intrusive source of annoyance. Thankfully they were never adopted over here and our grounds remain blissfully vuvuzela-free and there have been very few sightings of the Jabulani since, much to the relief of Robert Green et al.

Spain arrived in South Africa as European Champions, their stylish tiki-taka football finally delivering some silverware after the team had promised so much in previous tournaments only to come up short. So when they lost their opening match, meekly surrendering to Switzerland, the customary doubts about their temperament were raised. This time they confounded the doubters by becoming the only country to win the World Cup having lost their first game.

Although their football was always pleasing to the eye they were never spectacular and the grand total of eight goals in their seven games is the lowest by any winning team. In fact they are the only team to lift the World Cup without reaching a double-figure goal tally and five countries scored more goals than Spain in South Africa. Furthermore as those goals were shared between just three players, David Villa, Andrés Iniesta and Carlos Puyol, the Spaniards became the World Cup winners with the lowest number of goal scorers.

The final against the Netherlands was certainly not a thing of beauty with the Dutch reverting back to the roughhouse tactics they had employed against Spain's Iberian neighbours Portugal in the previous tournament. The yellow card count fell short of the Battle of Nuremberg but only just, with 14 bookings plus one red card for Johnny Heitinga making it the dirtiest final to date. Just like Arthur Ellis in the Battle of Berne in 1954 and Ken Aston in the Battle of Santiago in 1962, it was an Englishman caught in the middle. Howard Webb had his hands full in trying to keep a sense of order and he drew a fair amount of flak for not punishing a high tackle from Nigel de Jong that took the wind out of Xabi Alonso's sails and a few other parts of his body midway through the first half. Webb admitted he made a mistake in only issuing de Jong with a yellow card, saying: "Having seen it from my armchair several times in slow motion later and from different angles I can see that it was a red-card offence." When a referee issues a *mea culpa* you know there has been a massive mistake.

The Dutch received widespread opprobrium for their agricultural approach with the most stinging rebuke coming from one of their own. Johan Cruyff was clearly displeased with the performance describing it in the harshest way possible. "This ugly, vulgar, hermetic, hardly eye-catching, hardly football style, yes it served the Dutch to unsettle Spain," he said. "If with this they got satisfaction, fine, but they ended up losing. They were playing anti-football." This was quite something coming from the greatest player the Netherlands had ever produced. The journey from 'Total Football' to 'Anti-Football' could not have been more painful for a purist like Cruyff as he had been responsible for introducing the Spanish to his idealistic way of playing when he took over at Barcelona.

DEBUTANTS

After the glut of debutants in 2006, Slovakia were the only team to be participating in a World Cup for the first time although they had previous experience when part of Czechoslovakia. Having drawn their opening game against a limited New Zealand side and having lost the second to Paraguay their fate lay in their meeting with the holders, Italy. Fortunately for them this was an Italian side that had not so much gone backwards since its triumph in Berlin but had switched to full self-destruct mode.

In what was the game of the first round, Slovakia coasted into a 2-0 lead with a Róbert Vittek double only for Antonio Di Natale to peg them back to 2-1. The Slovaks scored their third in 89th minute through Kamil Kopúnek, swiftly followed by an Italian goal in added time by Fabio Quagliarella. Slovakia's win was orchestrated by the skilful captain Marek Hamšík who, with shades of Ahn Jung-Hwan's exploits in 2002, was the only player in Slovakia's starting XI playing his club football in Italy, for Napoli. Much to Italy's chagrin this was the only time in their 18 World Cup appearances that they ended up bottom of their group, with only two draws to show for their endeavours. Slovakia's 3-2 win assured them of a second-round berth against eventual finalists the Netherlands, which they lost narrowly 2-1.

HOME NATIONS

As had become the norm in recent tournaments, England were on their own as far as the home nations were concerned. Fabio Capello's team won the first nine of their 10 qualification games, only losing the dead rubber against Ukraine. However, that form did not translate into the tournament proper and a couple of incidents at either end of their campaign summed up the slightly hapless nature of life under Fabio Capello. The opening match paired England with their previous nemesis the USA but the expectations were that this was the perfect opportunity to lay rest the demons of Belo Horizonte as well as the failure qualify for 1994. All seemed to be going to plan when Steven Gerrard made a breakthrough after four minutes but then a shot out of the blue threw everything into disarray.

There seemed to be little danger when Clint Dempsey lined up a left-foot shot from outside the area and even less so when the American striker did not quite catch it right. His shot lacked any real venom and was pretty much straight at Robert Green who would surely just gather it in with the minimum of fuss and move on. Green duly bent down to collect the ball, which somehow squirmed through his grasp and spun towards the goal chased by the forlorn keeper who ended up in a heap of shame and humiliation. The ball dribbled over the line barely reaching the net as it nestled almost apologetically against it. The mortified Green was prostrate, no doubt looking intently for a hole to swallow him up.

Had the curse of the Jabulani struck or was it just an absolute howler? Capello clearly felt it was the latter as for the next game against Algeria, Green was replaced by David James who, at just the wrong side of 40, became the oldest World Cup debutant. While James kept a clean sheet the performance was nothing to celebrate and Wayne Rooney did not take well to the justifiable displeasure of the fans. A single goal victory over Slovenia in England's final game set up a meeting with England's other nemesis Germany.

Although England were pummelled into submission by a far superior team in nearly every aspect of the game there will always be one incident that everyone remembers. Finding themselves two goals down after 32 minutes, England clawed their way back into the game through a Matthew Upson goal on 37 minutes. Just 53 seconds later a long-range effort from Frank Lampard cannoned down from the crossbar at least two yards over the line before it spun back onto the field of play. From nowhere it seemed England were level just before half-time but the match officials waved play on. It remains a mystery how such a clear-cut case was missed and while Germany's keeper Manuel Neuer could hardly believe his luck, there was widespread condemnation. However, the Germans took a different view, claiming that this was retribution for Geoff Hurst's disputed goal in the 1966 final.

There has been countless speculation as to what might have happened if the scores had been 2-2 at half-time but the truth is that the Germans would probably still have won and if Lampard's goal had stood the final score would have been 4-2, an exact reverse of the Wembley final, now that would have been karma. England's inglorious exit was conveniently buried beneath the deluge of controversy. One good thing that came out of this kerfuffle was that the previous dilly-dallying over the use of goal-line technology was finally put to bed. Even Sepp Blatter admitted to FIFA's embarrassment over Lampard's ghost goal and so the technology was introduced for 2014 tournament. France became the first nation to benefit, against Honduras, when video technology showed that Noel Valladares fumbled Karim Benzema's shot over the line for an own goal.

FOOTNOTE

Of all the animals connected with the World Cup, be they real canines like Garrincha's dog and good old Pickles, or a figment of somebody's fevered imagination, such as World Cup Willie or Footix the smiling cockerel who graced the 1998 finals, perhaps the strangest and certainly the most psychic was Paul the octopus. Paul rose to fame as the accuracy of his predictions put many so-called experts and pundits to shame. Having warmed up in the European Championships in 2008 (when he got a reasonable five out of eight right) he correctly called each of Germany's seven matches in 2010 plus picked Spain for the final, appropriately for an eight-limbed creature giving him a 100% record from his eight predictions.

For those sceptics who suggested the success rate was a result of plain old probability rather than divination, the chances of predicting all eight results was 1/256. Amid the media hype there was talk of documentaries, endorsement deals and as usual wherever football is concerned, agents hovered, never too far away with lucrative offers, unfortunately Paul did not have long to enjoy or cash in on his hard-earned fame as he died a few months after the final.

2014

HOST
Brazil

CITIES
Belo Horizonte, Brasilia, Cuibaba, Curitiba, Fortaleza, Manaus,
Natal, Porto Alegre, Recife, Rio De Janeiro, Salvador, Sao Paolo

DEBUTANTS (1)
Bosnia-Herzegovina

FINAL
Sunday 13 July, Maracana Stadium, Rio de Janeiro (74,738)

ARGENTINA (0) 0 0
V
GERMANY (0) 0 1
Gotze
(After extra time)

TOTAL ATTENDANCE
3,429,873 over 64 matches (Average 53,592)

TOP GOALSCORER (6)
James Rodríguez, Colombia

"WHO IS RESPONSIBLE WHEN THE TEAM PLAYS? I AM. IT'S ME. WHO DECIDED THE TACTICS, I DID. SO THE PERSON RESPONSIBLE IS ME. IF I WERE TO THINK OF MY LIFE AS A PLAYER, AS A COACH, AS A TEACHER, THIS WAS THE WORST DAY OF MY LIFE. I'LL BE REMEMBERED PROBABLY BECAUSE I LOST 7-1, THE WORST DEFEAT BRAZIL HAVE EVER HAD."

Luiz Felipe Scolari takes responsibility for the Brazilians' calamitous semi-final defeat.

INTRODUCTION

The return of the World Cup to Brazil was heralded as the ultimate homecoming for the nation that, with five victories to its name, had more than anyone else. The aggregate attendance of just under 3.5 million was the second highest after USA 1994 and the average of 53,592 spectators for each match showed how much the tournament meant to Brazilians who anticipated righting the wrongs of their previous hosting of the tournament when Uruguay were crowned champions at their expense. Just like in 1950 things did not turn out quite as hoped for Brazil. In fact they were even worse as they suffered the humiliation of the largest ever World Cup semi-final defeat at the hands of Germany, who went on to win the tournament and close to within one of the *Seleção's* record.

Gary Lineker was moved to say of the hosts' 7-1 defeat: "In nigh on half a century of watching football, that's the most extraordinary, staggering, bewildering game I've ever witnessed." We all knew what he meant and we watched with increasing incredulity as Germany mercilessly ripped the sorry Brazilians apart in Belo Horizonte, scene of England's ignominious defeat to the USA when Brazil were last hosts. The absence of Neymar and Thiago Silva had weakened the Brazilians but should not have done so to this extent. The over-wrought pre-match tributes to Neymar, who had been injured in the quarter-final, at least got everyone prepared for the tears that flowed afterwards.

It got so bad it almost felt as if we were prying on the grief of a nation. Alongside the copious tears there was also the collective shaking of heads in sheer disbelief that this could happen. The Germans were as ruthless as the Brazilians were pathetic and in the course of the demolition Miroslav Klose scored his 16th World Cup goal, overtaking the record of Brazil's Ronaldo. Klose's goal ushered in a dizzying spell of four German goals in the space of six minutes and before the half hour mark they were five goals to the good. The fourth and fifth goals were the height of embarrassment as the Germans played untroubled one-twos in the penalty area before slotting home. It was as if they were completing a training drill with no serious opposition. When the sixth goal went in Germany edged ahead of Brazil as the highest scorers in the World Cup history.

To further underline the scale of this humiliation it was Brazil's heaviest World Cup defeat with the 3-0 loss to France in the 1998 World Cup final a close run affair by comparison. It was also Brazil's first competitive loss at home for 39 years. When Oscar scored the most pointless goal in Brazilian football history in the last minute the crowd cheered with as much sarcasm as they could muster. They had already turned on their heroes and had been acknowledging their conquerors for every pass completed and even cheered the seventh goal in a stinging rebuke to the players who had let them down so alarmingly. When Brazil followed this with a 3-0 loss to the Dutch in the third-place play-off it meant they had conceded as many goals in two games as they had done in the knock-out stages of the previous four tournaments, dating back to 1998. Finally, to complete their misery they had not lost two games consecutively since 1974.

Brazil were not the only former winners to experience humiliating defeat. The holders Spain suffered a calamitous 5-1 defeat in their opening match against the Netherlands. This was the first time previous finalists had met again in their first game of the following tournament. After Xabi Alonso stroked home an early penalty expectations were that the pre-tournament favourites would continue the momentum that had seen them win not just the last World Cup but also the last two European Championships.

Rather than being intimidated and resorting to the brutalism of four years previously, the Dutch responded with a performance of brio and brilliance. Robin van Persie's equaliser on the stroke of half-time was the pick of the bunch as he sailed through the air to meet Daley Blind's enticing cross before looping a header over a stranded Iker Casillas. It was the first goal the Spaniards had conceded in five World Cup games and after the break the game turned into one of the most unexpected routs. Led by Arjen Robben, who twinkled and turned his way through a vulnerable Spanish defence to score twice, the Dutch added another four goals to inflict the heaviest ever defeat suffered by reigning champions.

A shell-shocked Spain could not recover in time for their second match, which they lost 2-0 to Chile, thus being eliminated before their third group game, the only time that the reigning champions had lost their first two games in the following competition. Spain were unrecognisable from the team that had conceded only two goals in South Africa, it was the limpest of title defences as they shipped seven in those two games. The champions were well and truly dethroned and one was left wondering what might have happened if the Dutch had adopted a similar approach in Johannesburg four years before. Spain joined Italy in 2010 and France in 2002 as champions who did not progress beyond the first round.

DEBUTANTS

As in 2010 there was only one team appearing for the first time, another of the Balkan countries, Bosnia and Herzegovina. Despite going behind to a Sead Kolašinac own goal in the opening minutes of their first game, against Argentina, they more than matched their opponents until Lionel Messi scored a majestic second-half goal. A late consolation from substitute Vedad Ibišević was the least Bosnia deserved from a spirited performance in which they had more attempted shots and also shots on target than their conquerors.

Needing to win their second game against Nigeria, Bosnia thought they had taken the lead through Edin Džeko but his effort was ruled offside and seven minutes later they were behind to a goal from Stoke's Peter Odemwingie. The defeat meant Bosnia were already out before their last group game. Against Iran they did come to life and finally started to convert some of their chances with Džeko and Miralem Pjanić putting them ahead before a couple of late goals for either side finished off the scoring. Iran's coach and erstwhile assistant at Manchester United Carlos Querioz was generous in his assessment of his opponent's impact: "The best team of the group did not qualify, Bosnia showed they have great players, a great team with a lot of experience."

HOME NATIONS

If Brazil and Spain faltered dramatically then England subsided meekly to the worst performance in their 14 appearances to date, they certainly did nothing to erase the memory of the Belo Horizonte nightmare. When England were drawn against Italy, Uruguay and Costa Rica, the FA chairman Greg Dyke responded by mock slitting of his throat. It was a spectacularly misjudged attempt at gallows humour albeit a prescient one. What Dyke did not realise when giving his all too candid assessment of the strength of their group was that the so-called minnows Costa Rica, who were in their fourth tournament, would top the group. In reaching the quarter-finals the Costa Ricans would go further than any of the more vaunted group opponents, who had amassed seven World Cup titles between them.

Dyke was not the only senior England official to make a faux pas with manager Roy Hodgson commenting that Manaus, the venue for their opener against Italy, was "not an ideal place to play football". Despite furious backtracking by Hodgson and the

FA's PR team the die was cast. Things did not get much better when the action switched to the pitch and a pair of 2-1 defeats to Italy in the opener and Uruguay in Sao Paulo coupled with Italy's defeat to Costa Rica meant that England were already out before the last group game, which was, by one of those twists of fate, in Belo Horizonte. They had failed to reach the second round for the first time since 1958, when they drew all three of their group games only to lose out to the Soviet Union in a play-off. The only other time they were eliminated in the first round was, of course, in 1950 in Brazil.

England could certainly not be accused of skimping on their preparations with a 72-strong entourage of psychiatrists, dieticians, even a turf specialist accompanying the players and coaching staff. Perhaps the moment that best summed up the dismal bleakness of the campaign was when Daniel Sturridge equalised in the Italy game the team physiotherapist Gary Lewin celebrated so excessively on the sidelines that he injured himself and had to be stretchered off in tragicomic ignominy. No other country has the knack of turning joy to despair with such panache. One crumb of comfort for England was that when Sturridge equalised he was only the second English Number 9 to score since 1966, the other being Alan Shearer in 1998. I did say it was a crumb and nothing more.

FOOTNOTE

This was Germany's eighth appearance in a final, more than any other team, and they have won half of those games. Their deserved victory over Argentina in Rio was the first time a European country had won the World Cup on the South American continent and also was the third successive European win – a unique continental hat-trick. This was despite the fact that only six European countries made the last 16, the lowest number of Europeans to reach the round of 16 since the format was introduced in 1986. It was also the third consecutive occasion that the final had gone to extra time.

This was Europe's 11th success compared to South America's nine and there have been almost twice as many European to South

American finalists at 26 and 14 respectively, so the balance of power is certainly on this side of the Atlantic for the time being. There has yet to be either an Asian or African country making the final with South Korea coming the closest when they reached the semi-finals in 2002. Whether the European/South American dominance will continue for the foreseeable future is open to question although the controversial decision to give the 2022 tournament to Qatar might be a factor.

There have only been eight countries that have won the World Cup and it is hard to see beyond that select group winning in Russia. Amazingly there have only been four other teams that have reached the final – Czechoslovakia 1934, 1962; Hungary 1938, 1954; the Netherlands 1974, 1978, 2010; Sweden 1958 - so just 12 countries have filled the 40 slots. Since 1970 just seven countries have reached a World Cup final, while ten other sides have made it to the semi-finals. Such a pattern suggests that experience is a significant advantage. The World Cup will always produce sensations, surprises and shocks but invariably the usual suspects will be left battling it out for the most sought-after prize in football.